LISTENING TO THE VOICE WITHIN

BECOMING ENLIGHTENED

SHAHAN SHAMMAS

WORTHWHILE PUBLICATIONS

ISBN: 9780966202823

Library of Congress Control Number: 2018675309
Printed in the United States of America

*To my wife, Barbara, and my daughters, Olivia and Emily,
and their husbands, Ben and Antony. To anyone ready
to wake up, be transformed and live to make a difference.*

CONTENTS

INTRODUCTION

What is The Voice Within?

I do not believe I am special. I was born in Aleppo, Syria to parents, who for all practical purposes, were illiterate! My father was very abusive, not because he was a mean person by nature, but as a result of his frustrations. He had 6 children and he could not keep a job. He was talented, had pride and a temper. He was a day worker who lost his job routinely due to his temper. Even when he worked, he did not earn enough to take care of his family. Hence, his rage and frustration. He poured out his anger on his family, mostly my mother and me.

My mother passed away at the age of 36. She left behind 6 children ranging in age from 3 to 15. Life became very difficult for us, almost intolerable. My dad had to face reality. His motto, "You have children and God will take care of them", was not working. He had to do something. He placed 3 of the youngest in orphanages, and gave me up to the Church to study and become a monk. He kept one child and sent the oldest away after a fight. I ended up in a monastery in Lebanon. The question that has always been on my mind, "Was that accidental? Or, is there more to it?"

I am in my early seventies now. Looking back, I can clearly see that nothing in my life was accidental.

All along, I had a hidden companion, a light that shone at critical junctures in my life and showed me the way. The choice was always mine. I could act, or I could ignore the urge. I discovered that the easiest, fastest way to grow and "make it" in life was to listen to *The Voice Within*. This voice was not intrusive, loud or demanding. It was clear, simple and unexpected. It was a "wild card" that appeared suddenly, and now I had an alternative, a real choice, and a decision to make.

As I said at the beginning, I am not special. I believe we each have something unique within us. It is a "piece" of God. The ancients referred to it as "the breath of life" or "the still small voice." Christ called it "the kingdom of God within you." He likened it to a "seed", "yeast", "hidden treasure", "fine pearl", and a "net". These are of central value, essential, and very significant.

I refer to what we have within us as *The Voice Within*. It is within us because we are the Word and the Work of God. This Voice Within is the spur to awaken and actualize "The Divine Potential" within each of us. To make this potential actual requires us to actively seek to grow by engaging with life and making the most of our experiences.

The Voice Within awakens at critical junctures in our lives. Once awake, it provides us with answers and guides our important decisions. To hear it, we must be open to its promptings. We must want its guidance. We must crave to hear its voice. We prepare for it, when we ask, seek, and knock.

Ask, and it will be given to you; seek, and you will find; knock, and it will be opened to you. For everyone who asks receives, and the one who seeks finds, and to the one who knocks it will be opened. Mark 7:7-8

Our asking must be in earnest, our seeking must be intense, and our knocking must be loud and persistent. The answer can come in a flash, and through any means. It can come through a person we meet, from a dream, or be triggered by a word we hear or read. Our **intention** to have an answer is the key that triggers *The Voice Within*.

We all want things, but do we always want what is best for us? Often, we do not; for we seek immediate gratification at the expense of our long-term good. Years ago, I made a pact with myself that regardless of what I ask for, I want the will of the Higher Self to be done. For me, it is always **Thy Will Be Done**. I do my part of asking, seeking, and knocking and then I let go. I have no attachment to outcomes, knowing that my Higher Self will always bring into my life what I need most.

It is impossible for me to accept that God can favor me or anyone else over another. Yet, we are all different. Some "appear" favored, while others do not. I believe we "favor" ourselves when we listen to *The Voice Within* and act on its promptings. It is absolutely critical to realize that *The Voice Within* is our own voice. We, as a complete being, have two selves: the normal everyday egoic self concerned with survival and bound by the Newtonian laws of physics, and a Higher Self that is quantum. Our quantum self operates outside the confines of space/time and that is where the voice comes from. Our Higher Self provides us with an option that we can choose. This option is often the best from a sea of possibilities. Acting on *The Voice Within* is the most direct path to landing the job of our dreams, attracting the love of our lives, finding the most appropriate home, and living to manifest our vast potential.

We can distinguish *The Voice Within* from the chatter of our thoughts and the voice of our ego by its fruit. It will never tell us, or order us to do anything, especially to harm another. This "voice" is a "knowing" from deep within of an option that if acted on, can provide new possibilities. These possibilities often lead to other possibilities and are never ends in themselves, more of a turn in direction that might require other turns before we arrive at our ultimate good. We are always free to act on the promptings of *The Voice Within* or not. Using our reason, feelings and inspiration, we can decide. Once we do, we are responsible for our choice. Additionally, there is no guarantee that we will succeed, for we can sabotage our own good at any time. The most important quality of *The Voice Within* is that it will be the truth and it will set us free.

I have heard and acted on *The Voice Within* numerous times and continue to do so. The first time I heard *The Voice Within* in the United States was in 1972. I was working in a plastics factory near Maynard, MA. I was listening to music playing on the radio. A commercial came on that said: **Be all you can be. Join the Army.** Instantly I knew that is what I should do. The very next day, I signed up for three years in the U.S. Army.

It was one of the best decisions that I have ever made. I signed up to be a Food Inspector. However, after several synchronicities and promptings from *The Voice Within*, I ended up working as an Electron Microscopist at the First US Army Laboratory at Ft. Meade, MD. From there I transferred to Walter Reed Army Medical Center in Washington, DC and then I transferred to the Treasury Department. These were some of the best decisions of my life.

The Voice Within is personal. Each of us has his or her own experiences with it. I can only comment about my experiences with *The Voice Within*. Some of my most important decisions or "knowings" were promptings from *The Voice Within*. Here are three more brief examples:

My Near-Death Experience

I knew clearly, completely and unequivocally that I was going to die. I was not sick and had not had any traumas. Prior to my near-death experience, *The Voice Within* made it clear to me what I needed to do before it was too late. I had a few days to prepare. When the event happened, I gained life-altering insights. I also realized that we, undeniably, have freedom of choice and that we are at the helm of our lives, if we so choose.

My Wife

During my first date with Barbara, while I was driving her home that night, she fell asleep in my car.

I stopped the car, took a blanket from the trunk, and covered her up. I knew at that moment that Barbara was going to be my wife. *The Voice Within* had spoken. How I met and ended up marrying Barbara is the result of my listening to *The Voice Within*.

This Book

The genesis of this book is due to synchronicity, for it was not my intention to write a book. My intention was to go to New Zealand without having to fly there. While my daughter, Emily, was in college, she arranged to go to the University of Auckland for a semester abroad. My wife went to Auckland to visit, but not me. She told me how beautiful and remote New Zealand was. I wanted to go there, but did not want to be on a plane for too many hours. I wanted to cruise there.

One day, early in 2018, I saw an advertisement for a world cruise. Instantly, I knew that was my opportunity to go to New Zealand. This was a prompting from *The Voice Within*. I consulted my wife and we booked the cruise. Before our departure on January 1, 2019, our daughter and her husband gave me a gift. It was a beautiful leather-bound journal. As soon as we entered our cabin, we saw two journals on our bed, a gift from the ship to my wife and me. Now I had an extra journal. What was I to do with the second journal? I decided to document my thoughts, and within a few weeks, I had written all the preliminary chapters of this book. This book is an example of synchronicity, inspiration and listening to *The Voice Within*.

On May 6, 2019, we returned home. Soon after, I started typing the material from my journal into my computer and after several iterations, *Listening to The Voice Within* was born. The purpose of *The Voice Within* is to guide our unfoldment and direct our maturation in the quickest and best way possible and to help us transform into enlightened beings. The underlying assumption is that we are here on earth to accomplish certain feats, to learn important lessons, and to have a positive impact on the world.

PART ONE

◆ ◆ ◆

THE JOURNEY BEGINS

THE JOURNEY

*Life is a journey that must be traveled no matter
how bad the roads and accommodations.*

— *Oliver Goldsmith*

A ll journeys start and end. They also have a destination. My life journey started when I was born and will end when I die. Like all journeys, it helps to have a destination in mind, or else how would we know when we arrive or when to make a turn. I can easily see the destination of my journey now that I am in my seventies. I started life as an infant, went through childhood, adolescence and finally adulthood. I have been an adult for quite a while now, yet my journey continues. Where am I heading? I believe I am on my way to maturity.

What is true of me, a human, is also true of humanity. Humanity has gone through the Stone Age, the Bronze Age, the Iron Age, the Industrial Age and is now in the Technological/Information Age. Stated differently, humanity has gone through infancy, childhood, adolescence, and is now poised for adulthood and maturity. These stages are not distinct and often overlap. Each developmental stage is necessary and vital in the process of our growth and maturation. Infancy is no more or less important than adulthood. Similarly, the Industrial Age is no more or less important than the

Technological Age. Each stage is based on the previous one and is the foundation for the next.

We are on a journey to maturity, both individually and collectively. On this journey, we can be heroes or cowards. The difference is a choice between courage and fear. Often, courage is action in spite of fear. Just as we are not expected to stagnate in any of these stages, so it is with humanity. We must continue to grow. The earlier the growth stage, the more supervision and guidance is required both for individuals and humanity. For a human, this supervision comes from parents, teachers, and other adults or authority figures. For humanity, this guidance and, at times, intervention came through gods, angels, prophets, seers, kings, and a few distinguished individuals, and even natural disasters such as hurricanes, tsunamis, floods, volcanoes and earthquakes.

One thing is absolutely certain. Our current journey will end. Keeping that in mind, we need to make this journey as impactful as we can and have fun in the process.

Infancy

I do not remember anything from my infancy. The earliest I can remember is when I was three and a half years old. Since my wife and I had our own children, I know a bit about this stage. Infancy is when we are in the dark, helpless, clueless and dependent. Infants require a great deal of patience, love and care. Parents have to supervise them constantly. Humanity, in its infancy, needed care and supervision as well. They had shamans, tribal leaders and kings for that. Primitive religions had a lot to teach early humanity. Humans had to learn cooperation in social groups, follow rules, abide by regulations and be obedient to higher authorities. Kings were usually despotic. The Code of Hammurabi is one of the earliest to enforce justice. It consists of 282 rules, establishing standards for commercial interactions, and setting fines and punishments to meet the requirements of justice.

Childhood

I remember more of my childhood. I mostly went to school and played soccer on the street with my friends. The only toy I ever had as a child was a small ball which I cherished. One day while on a visit to a blind relative, I could not find my ball. I looked for the ball everywhere to no avail. I started to cry. My blind relative comforted me and promised me that she would find the ball once the adults drank their Turkish coffee and she read their cups. Once done with the coffee, she started reading one of the cups and told me exactly where the ball was. She, however, never told me that she was the one who hid it there in the first place. I was so glad to have my ball back that it never occurred to me how a blind person could read a coffee cup.

Childhood for a human is a time for play, a time to grow strong and gain confidence. While a human gains confidence through play, humanity did it by playing with fire – through wars. Whereas a human child is watched over by parents and the family, humanity had kings, priests and prophets. Humans were given commandments, rules about how to live and what is or is not acceptable. They were controlled by fear of punishment, if they strayed and by rewards, if they complied. The Old Testament is replete with these. An early move toward establishing a boundary between the rulers and the ruled was the Magna Carta signed by the King of England in 1215. The Magna Carta aided our growth by granting the rights of all free citizens to own and inherit property and to be protected from excessive taxes.

Adolescence

My mother passed away when I was 13. After a week of attention from one of my Aunts, all care-giving stopped. I was on my own. I dropped out of school and got a job working at my uncle's bakery in Aleppo, Syria. One day I was helping a worker deliver pita bread to a restaurant when we had a terrible accident. He had a large crate of stacked bread on the motorbike handle, while I held onto him from behind. He got distracted talking to me and went straight at an oncoming car. I was severely injured, but eventually I recovered. After this accident, an adult relative helped enroll me in a Catholic Technical School run by Italian monks. This is where I gave my first confession. After the priest asked me several questions about sins that I might have committed, I began to think that I should admit to at least one sin, or else there won't be anything to confess. So, to the next question, my answer was yes. The priest sounded startled and asked me again: you have committed adultery? I answered that I did not know what that word meant.

For a human, adolescence is the period of transition between childhood and adulthood. It includes changes in the way we relate to the world, increased decision-making, facing pressures, and a search for identity. As an adolescent humanity, we needed guidance and moral codes to better relate to each other, rules of behavior to help our decision-making, and a reward-punishment system to nudge us in the desired direction. We received these through our religions, laws, agreements and treaties.

Adulthood

I became an adult in the United States when I had a real job earning good money and was able to independently take care of myself. This occurred when I enlisted in the U.S. Army for three years. I paid back a college loan and bought my first car. I was fully responsible for my life.

For a human, adulthood is when our abilities are at their peak, including our intelligence, memory, and reasoning. Adulthood is when we become more independent and assume greater responsibilities. I know when I became an adult. It is not as easy to say the same about humanity. In many ways, many countries still behave as adolescents. However, there are some leaders and countries that act like adults. These countries have well established constitutions, political systems, and an independent judiciary system. Humanity continues to move toward adulthood through the contributions of exceptional individuals. Through their passion, dedication and uniqueness, these individuals pushed humanity forward, to adulthood. These outstanding individuals include many scientists and spiritual leaders such as: Christ, the U.S. Founding Fathers, Louis Pasteur, Jonas Polk, Einstein, Mahatma Gandhi, and Martin Luther King, Jr.

Maturity

My journey to maturity was guided by *The Voice Within*. While in the U.S. Army, I discovered the writings of Wilhelm Reich and read them all. I then happened upon the writings of Jane Roberts and read all of her books. In February of 1972, I joined the Rosicrucian Order, AMORC (The Ancient and Mystical Order Rosae Crucis) and began studying their teachings which lasted more than 30 years. Beginning in 1975, I also began teaching and public speaking. I constantly read and study diverse subjects to expand my mind and add to my knowledge base. I am continuously edging closer to maturity.

A mature person is able to keep long-term commitments, is unshaken by flattery or criticism, and is humble. Humility isn't thinking less of oneself; it is thinking of oneself less. A mature person's decisions are based on character, not feelings. Mature people live governed by values. They have principles that guide their decisions. A mature person expresses gratitude consistently. A mature person acts responsibly instead of reacts and seeks knowledge, wisdom and understanding.

A mature humanity eschews barbarism in the form of war, aggression, dominance and elitism. A mature humanity espouses cooperation, creativity, individuality and tolerance. A mature humanity places service ahead of selfishness and more value on health, happiness and productivity than on profit. While infancy is the beginning of the journey of humanity, maturity is the end of one journey and the beginning of another, a journey to establish peace on earth, to transform ourselves and our world into a paradise of our choosing.

Just as I did not grow from infancy to adulthood without supervision and at times intervention, it was the same with humanity. My supervision was evident in the acts of the adults in my life. Supervision for humanity was more subtle. We can detect it through the directives of gods, demigods, kings and prophets. Their aim was to keep us in line. Intervention, on the other hand, was more blunt, decisive and impactful. It altered the trajectory of my life and the course of history for humanity. Here are a few examples.

Examples of Intervention

In my journey to maturity, I experienced several changes in course via, what appears to be, "interventions" which re-directed the path of my life. A poignant example is how I managed to go to college. After graduating from high school and earning my baccalaureate degree from the Lebanese Government, I applied for and took the entrance exam to attend the American University of Beirut (AUB). I had no money and no one to borrow the needed funds from. My Aunt, an

American missionary who was the only one who could have helped, declined. She informed me that God did not want me to go to college based on all the available evidence. I became extremely angry and stormed out of her place. Outside, as I was walking in fury, I heard someone calling for me. I stopped. It was Jean, an American lady I barely knew. After talking with me, she invited me to her house to further discuss my options for how I could go to college. When I met her in her house, after some discussions, we realized quickly that I did not have any options. So she handed me enough cash to pay for the first semester. She told me she was confident that I would be able to secure a scholarship after the first semester. I attended, and graduated from, the American University of Beirut. An unexpected intervention indeed. This is only one example that altered the trajectory of my life.

There were also several direct interventions in the course of human history to ensure that humans stayed on course to grow, develop and continue to progress to maturity. What constitutes evidence for some is merely circumstantial for others. We are free to believe whatever we choose. It is undeniable, though, that our religions are full of descriptions, or stories of interventions. All three Abrahamic religions portray angels. Angels are messengers from the gods. They played major roles in shaping our beliefs and directing the course of humanity.

Here are a few specific examples:

Judaism

Abraham

There is a lot we can question, discuss or argue about in Judaism, and not reach a consensus. Did Moses part the Red Sea? Was Jonah swallowed by a whale? Did Adam and Eve ever exist? Does God actually appear and talk to people? I do not know the answers to any of these questions. I do know, however, that there are many instances that count as evidence that something extraordinary has taken place, or an intervention occurred that redirected the course of humanity. I will only use a few scenarios. For example:

> *Now the LORD said to Abram, "Go from your country and your kindred and your father's house to the land that I will show you.*
>
> *Genesis 12:1-2*

Why would a seventy-five-year-old man, Abram, take Sarai, his wife, and Lot, his brother's son, and all their possessions and go to a new land, some place completely new and unknown to them? Who exactly was this Lord who commanded Abram to leave? Was the command in human language? Why did Abram do as he was told? The fact that he did is evidence that something actually took place to make Abram comply. This is a clear case of intervention in human affairs to redirect the course of history.

Abraham And Isaac

According to the Bible, God was testing Abraham's faith when he asked him to sacrifice his only son Isaac. I have no idea how God communicated with Abraham. If I had heard a voice asking me to sacrifice my child, I would have said, in reply to the voice, what Jesus said to Peter when Peter tried to thwart Christ from His mission: "Get behind me, you Satan" (Matthew 16:23).

> *After these things God tested Abraham and said to him, "Abraham!" And he said, "Here I am." He said, "Take your son, your only son Isaac, whom you love, and go to the land of Moriah, and offer him there as a burnt offering on one of the mountains of which I shall tell you." So Abraham rose early in the morning, saddled his donkey, and took two of his young men with him, and his son Isaac. And he cut the wood for the burnt offering and arose and went to the place of which God had told him.*
>
> *Genesis 22:1-3*

Abraham was determined to sacrifice his only son, Isaac. He did not hesitate, or question the demand. I know of no sane parent who would ever consider carrying out such an act. Perhaps what Abraham experienced was compelling and extraordinary. If Abraham had completed what he was intending on doing, the course of history would have been altered. Was this a test of faith or sanity? Is this account to teach us blind obedience to authority? Is this how we were trained to give up our freedom of choice and control of our lives to "those who know better"? Is this the start of blind faith?

Moses

Moses was not an articulate man. He describes himself as not being eloquent, slow of speech and having a slow tongue. Yet, he was chosen to change the course of human history.

> *But Moses said to the LORD, "Oh, my Lord, I am not eloquent, either in the past or since you have spoken to your servant, but I am slow of speech and of tongue."*   *Exodus 4:10*

God appears to Moses:

> *Now Moses was keeping the flock of his father-in-law, Jethro, the priest of Midian, and he led his flock to the west side of the wilderness and came to Horeb, the mountain of God. And the angel of the LORD appeared to him in a flame of fire out of the midst of a bush. He looked, and behold, the bush was burning, yet it was not consumed. And Moses said, "I will turn aside to see this great sight, why the bush is not burned." When the LORD saw that he turned aside to see, God called to him out of the bush, "Moses, Moses!" And he said, "Here I am." Then he said, "Do not come near; take your sandals off your feet, for the place on which you are standing is holy ground." And he said, "I am the God of your*

*father, the God of Abraham, the God of Isaac,
and the God of Jacob." And Moses hid his face,
for he was afraid to look at God. Exodus 3:1-6*

Who was the angel of the Lord who appeared
to Moses in the burning bush? Who was the one who
called himself *"I am the God of your father, the God of
Abraham, the God of Isaac, and the God of Jacob"*? Is the
angel God? Did he speak to Moses in Aramaic or Hebrew? Moses' experience must have been so powerful
and convincing that he gave up his way of life and did
as he was told. He became fearless in confronting the
Pharaoh of Egypt. Moses was raised in the house of the
Pharaoh, yet he turned against him. Why? This is another example of intervention in human affairs which
changed the course of history.

There are many interventions by gods, angels
or demigods in several of the ancient religions. Taking sides so one group can defeat another is a familiar
story in the Bible and in ancient Indian traditions. The
drowning of the Egyptian army in the Red Sea after the
parting of the sea by Moses is one such example. Here is
another example of a direct intervention:

*And that night the angel of the LORD went out
and struck down 185,000 in the camp of the
Assyrians. And when people arose early in the
morning, behold, these were all dead bodies.*

2 Kgs 19:35

Christianity

Paul

We can argue about the nature of Christ, whether he was a man, a god or both. We can also discuss if he was a mere prophet or the Son of God. We can debate his birth from a virgin, whether or not he died and rose from the dead. Was he, in fact, able to revive the dead? Did he walk on water? We can even question if he ever existed as a historical person. We will never know the answers to these questions beyond a shadow of a doubt. Even though many events can be questionable, there are two events that are difficult to dismiss. The first event involves Paul, who was Saul.

> *But Saul, still breathing threats and murder against the disciples of the Lord, went to the high priest and asked him for letters to the synagogues at Damascus, so that if he found any belonging to the Way, men or women, he might bring them bound to Jerusalem. Now as he went on his way, he approached Damascus, and suddenly a light from heaven shone around him. And falling to the ground he heard a voice saying to him, "Saul, Saul, why are you persecuting me?" And he said, "Who are you, Lord?" And he said, "I am Jesus, whom you are persecuting. But rise and enter the city, and you will be told what you are to do." The men who were traveling with him stood speechless, hearing the voice but seeing no one. Saul rose from the ground, and al-*

though his eyes were opened, he saw nothing. So
they led him by the hand and brought him into
Damascus. And for three days he was without
sight, and neither ate nor drank.   Acts 9:1-9

How can we explain the conversion of a man
known for his persecution of Christians – on his way
to Damascus to persecute even more – to make a complete U-turn and become a defender of Christians? In
fact, he became the creator of Christianity as we know
it. Something extraordinary must have happened to
Saul on his way to Damascus. This is undeniable and
constitutes evidence of interference. Saul transformed
from being a persecutor to Paul, a whole-hearted true
Christian. He even gave his life for his new beliefs. He
must have had a very unusual experience that redirected the course of humanity.

Constantine

"Constantine reigned during the 4th century CE
and is known for attempting to Christianize the Roman
Empire. He made the persecution of Christians illegal
by signing the Edict of Milan in 313 A.D. and helped
spread the religion by bankrolling church-building
projects, commissioning new copies of the Bible, and
summoning councils of theologians to hammer out the
religion's doctrinal kinks." (Paraphrased from the Bri-
tannica.)

How can we explain the conversion of a Roman
Emperor, known for his persecution of Christians, to
make a complete about-face and become a Christian
himself? In fact, he was the consolidator of the Christian Bible as we know it. Something extraordinary

must have happened to Constantine. It did. In 312 A.D., on the night before a decisive battle for control of the Western Roman Empire, Constantine claimed to have had a vision of a cross of light in the sky bearing the command. "In this sign, you will conquer." He did conquer. Does this constitute evidence of another interference? Constantine was transformed from being a persecutor to being a defender and a promoter of Christianity. He must have had a very unusual experience to make him reverse course. With his consolidation of Christianity, he redirected the course of humanity.

Islam

According to biographies of Muhammad, while on retreat in a mountain cave near Mecca, Gabriel appears before Muhammad and commands him to "Read!". He responded, "But I cannot read!". Then the angel Gabriel embraced him tightly and revealed to him the first lines of chapter 96 of the Qur'an, "Read: In the name of thy Lord Who createth, Createth man from a clot. Read: And thy Lord is the Most Bounteous, Who teacheth by the pen, Teacheth man that which he knew not" (Bukhari 4953).

Who was Gabriel? An angel? What does an angel look like? How does he communicate with humans? Is this the same Gabriel who appeared to Mary, the mother of Jesus? Why did he interfere and redirect the course of history? This is more evidence of meddling in human affairs and changing the course of our history so that we may continue to grow and evolve.

Natural Calamities

Our planet has experienced several natural calamities that shaped the course of human history. It is impossible to know if they were mere freak accidents or if there is more to it. Had it not been for the meteorite that struck earth and caused the demise of the dinosaurs, we would not be here. The great flood, as recorded by many ancient cultures, decimated humanity and history. The meteorite gave humanity a chance to evolve, while the great flood gave humanity a fresh start.

Here are two specific examples:

Genghis Khan

Genghis Khan, born as Temüjin Borjigin, was a 13th-century warrior in central Asia who founded the Mongol Empire, one of the largest empires in history. In the movie *Mogul*, a decisive battle was about to be waged, one in which Genghis Khan would have been defeated for sure, had it not been for a freak storm that appeared unexpectedly. The thunder and lightning instilled great fear in the hearts of the enemy soldiers. Genghis Khan, however, was unafraid. He won the admiration of the enemy soldiers and they pledged allegiance to him. He won that battle without a fight. Where did this storm, that turned events around, come from at a critical moment in history? Is this another intervention in human affairs to direct the course of history in a certain way? It sure looks like it.

The Spanish Armada

The Spanish Armada was a fleet of 130 ships that sailed from Corunna in late May 1588, under the command of the Duke of Medina Sidonia, with the purpose of escorting an army from Flanders to invade England. The Armada was difficult to attack because it sailed in a 'crescent' shape. While the Armada tried to get in touch with the Spanish army, the English ships attacked fiercely. However, an important reason why the English were able to defeat the Armada was that the wind blew the Spanish ships northwards. To many English people this proved that God wanted them to win and there were pictures and medals made to celebrate this fact. (paraphrased from The National Archives). It certainly appears as if the gods do want certain nations to win in order for progress to continue. The Spanish Armada was supposed to be invincible, yet it was destroyed by England. Another intervention? Perhaps.

Wild Card

There is one individual from ancient times who also exemplifies adulthood. He was way ahead of his time, yet had an impact, nevertheless.

Akhenaten

Born Amenhotep, in 1352 BC, Akhenaten ascended to the throne after his father died. Akhenaten abandoned traditional Egyptian polytheism and introduced monotheism centered on the worship of the one god Aten, represented by the sun disc. He claimed, "There is only one god, my father. I can approach him by day, by night." He felt that God was guiding him to make changes. He also wrote one of the most beautiful hymns of praise to Aten.

Akhenaten did the unthinkable for those times. He abandoned all military campaigns and dramatically scaled down Egypt's military defenses. He focused on the family and even elevated the status of his wife, Nefertiti, to be equal to him. Akhenaten instituted changes in art and culture directing artists to depict him and his family as they really were, with elongated skulls, long necks, sunken eyes, thick thighs, a potbelly- and female-like breasts. According to Egyptian Mythology, Akhenaten descended from the gods who arrived from the stars on Earth at the time of Zep Tepi. Zep Tepi refers to "First Time", a remote epoch prior to ancient Egypt. (paraphrased from Live Science).

What happened to Akhenaten to transform him into a reformist like no other in ancient history? Where did he get the belief that his origin was from the stars? Was he a wild card introduced to implant novel ideas into humanity and to drop seeds that would take centuries to mature?

The Next Stage

Independence and the March to Full Maturity

The only journey is the one within.

—*Rainer Maria Rilke*

When we were infants, our parents took care of us. They chose our food and even fed us, especially our beliefs. They set the boundaries for us as to what we can and cannot do. This is what happened with humanity. Judaism gave us rules that we needed when we were young. As we grew older, Christianity taught us love, acceptance of all, forgiveness, and service. Later, Islam taught us to surrender to the will of God. Natural calamities and historical figures made sure that we continued to unfold in a way that is best for humanity. Finally, to continue our journey to independence and full maturity, we must make a major shift. We must move from external authority to internal, personal authority. We must migrate from needing supervision and guidance to independence. We must prepare our own "food" and decide what we choose to believe. We must transition from submitting to the will of an external deity to listening to *The Voice Within*; from having the word of God in books to being the word and work of God ourselves. The kingdom and power of God is within us. We have direct access to deity. We have the power to create our own Garden of Eden. It is time to have the light within show us the way. It is time to listen to *The Voice Within* and live as mature adults.

LIFE AS AN EXPERIMENT

*Don't be too timid and squeamish about your
actions. All life is an experiment.*

— *Ralph Waldo Emerson*

When I first read about Adam and Eve in the Garden of Eden, I could not understand why God would place a good-looking tree in the middle of the garden and then ask the humans not to eat from it. Why not place the tree in a far corner instead? Was this a test of obedience? Or, was this an experiment to find out what humans would do with their freedom of choice?

Adam and Eve were in a predicament as to what action to take. What if all of humanity is in the same situation? Is it possible that we are in a new Garden of Eden, Earth, and that we are subjects in an equivalent experiment to find out:

1. How do we choose to use our freedom of choice? Will we ignore this gift or exercise it, and to what end?

2. Will we learn how to be happy?

3. Will we discover and use our talents and abilities, both obvious and latent?

4. Will we remember and get to know who we really are?

5. How well will we care for our garden, the earth, ourselves and each other?

An experiment cannot have a predetermined outcome. The outcome cannot be prejudiced by the expectations of the experimenter. It cannot be judged as good or bad. The results are simply accepted and used to further our knowledge.

How do we choose to use our freedom of choice? Will we ignore this gift or exercise it, and to what end?

We are expected to exercise our freedom of choice to, at a minimum, double the expertise, talents and abilities that we started with. The best way we can do this is to discover and live our passions, and place our talents and abilities in loving service of others.

Will we learn how to be happy?

Some say that the purpose of life is to live and to be happy. How, then, can we be happy? I have discovered that happiness is the result of making others happy through love and service, the essence of Christianity.

*Will we discover and use
our talents and abilities,
both obvious and latent?*

We come to this world under varying circumstances with different gifts and challenges, both latent and obvious. Some of us are given very little to start with, while others have much more. Regardless, the object of the experiment is the same. What will we do with our lot? The only requirement is that we cannot be slothful (lazy). This is alluded to in The **Parable of the Talents**:

For it will be like a man going on a journey, who called his servants and entrusted to them his property. To one he gave five talents, to another two, to another one, to each according to his ability. Then he went away. He who had received the five talents went at once and traded with them, and he made five talents more. So also he who had the two talents made two talents more. But he who had received the one talent went and dug in the ground and hid his master's money. Now after a long time the master of those servants came and settled accounts with them. And he who had received the five talents came forward, bringing five talents more, saying, 'Master, you delivered to me five talents; here I have made five talents more.' His master said to him, 'Well done, good and faithful servant. You have been faith-

ful over a little; I will set you over much. Enter into the joy of your master.' And he also who had the two talents came forward, saying, 'Master, you delivered to me two talents; here I have made two talents more.' His master said to him, 'Well done, good and faithful servant. You have been faithful over a little; I will set you over much. Enter into the joy of your master.' He also who had received the one talent came forward, saying, 'Master, I knew you to be a hard man, reaping where you did not sow, and gathering where you scattered no seed, so I was afraid, and I went and hid your talent in the ground. Here you have what is yours.' But his master answered him, 'You wicked and slothful servant! You knew that I reap where I have not sown and gather where I scattered no seed? Then you ought to have invested my money with the bankers, and at my coming I should have received what was my own with interest. So take the talent from him and give it to him who has the ten talents. For to everyone who has will more be given, and he will have an abundance. But from the one who has not, even what he has will be taken away. And cast the worthless servant into the outer darkness. In that place there will be weeping and gnashing of teeth.'

Matt 25:14-30

Some of us discover our talents early on. Others have to wait. Some talents and skills are natural and inherited, while others must be cultivated. Some abilities are independent and stand on their own, such as music and athleticism, while others are composite and require other factors to be developed prior to their manifestation. A skill such as being a successful business owner requires several cultivated abilities. The easiest path to discover our talents is to follow our passions.

Will we remember and get to know who we really are?

A human being is composed of about 100 trillion cells. Each cell is endowed with the same chromosomes – genetic material and DNA. Hence, each cell can, potentially and actually, develop into a whole human.

What if we separate the cells, place them in different environments, and give them freedom of choice? Then we can observe them. We can determine how long it will take them to attain their full potential of becoming the whole body and manifesting all of its abilities. Once separated, the cells forget that they were part of the whole, the body. The abilities of the body are gone. The individual cells can no longer think, speak, sing, run, cook or paint. These are mere potentials now and must be re-developed.

We are like the individual cells, separated from our source and given freedom of choice. How long will it take us to re-member and know our source/origin, which is also our destination? To re-member is to rejoin the family of which we were a part, a member. The question is not *if* we will re-member since it is only a matter of time. The question becomes, which path will we take to get there? Will we follow the path of least resistance, allow others to determine a path for us, or will we chart our own course?

How long would it take us to grow, mature and realize our full potential? Having freedom, how will we act? What choices will we make? Will we analyze the consequences of our choices prior to acting?

*How well will we care
for our garden, the earth,
ourselves and each other?*

Will we assume responsibility for our well-being, the health of the planet, and contribute to the welfare of others? Or, will we simply live to gratify ourselves, plunder the earth's resources and take advantage of others?

I was recently on a cruise ship travelling around the world for 120 days. Breakfast, lunch and dinner were available in the buffet or in one of the restaurants. Water, tea and coffee were free of charge. All other drinks had to be purchased. There were also specialty restaurants where one could purchase food.

The ship I was on was like a miniature world. We had an opportunity to exercise our freedom of choice and choose. We could eat anything, and as much as we liked. We could have any type of drinks. We could relax and enjoy free time or we could choose to take excursions. No choice was good or bad, right or wrong. Each came with specific results and consequences. How would we choose to act? Would we be guided by whims, succumb to appetite, follow the actions of others? Or, would we take charge, exercise choice and do what is best for us? Would our choices hinder or advance our personal, spiritual unfoldment, the opening of our eyes, and our progress to full self-actualization? It is our choice to do with our lives as we see fit. Being aware of the consequences prior to exercising our will, however, is a great advantage. Unlike scientific experiments that can succeed or fail, the experiment of life is always a success. For it is we who plan and execute this experiment. The end result is always the same – growth and maturation. What varies is how we get there and how long it takes us to arrive.

FREE WILL

As far as I can see, it's not important that we have free will, just as long as we have the illusion of free will to stop us going mad.

— *Alan Moore*

When I was in high school, I started reading many philosophy books. I was especially fascinated by the writings of Frederick Nietzsche. My best friend Elias and I were both interested in philosophy. We used to take long walks and discuss deep subjects.

One subject we discussed was free will. Do we have free will or do we act as the result of memory, reflex, cause and effect? I sided with having free will. As we were walking, I saw an empty can on the road. I told my friend: I can choose to kick this can or not. My decision would be based on free will, for it matters not whether I kick it or not. I would not be seeking pleasure or attempting to avoid pain. There are no memories in my mind to guide my decision, and instinct plays no role in this choice. At times, when I am preparing food, I fill two plates with food and hold one in each hand. I then ask my wife, who is in another room, which hand she prefers. She has no reason to choose one or the other. Her choice is an exercise of free will.

I know that some do not believe that we have free will. They believe that we behave based on instinct and programmed behavior. I believe otherwise. For me, freedom of choice is a trademark of being human. Regardless, a better question might be: if we have free will, how many of us actually use it, how often, and toward what purpose? The story of Adam and Eve is about freedom of choice. We all have it. Having something is not the same as using it wisely.

What determines if we exercise our freedom of choice? How "free" is our freedom of choice? If we have something in abundance and seldom use it, how good is it? Let us suppose that we have a million dollars in the bank and we only use $50,000 of it over our lifetime. Does it matter that we had a million dollars? Use determines value.

Adam and Eve had it easy. They had one choice to make: resist temptation or give in to it. We, on the other hand, are surrounded by an ocean of choices. We can choose to use our time as a precious resource, or waste it. We can choose to invest our money for positive benefits, or squander it. We can choose to cultivate our skills and abilities for maximum results, or we can let them remain dormant. We can choose to study, learn and improve, or we can choose not to. We can decide to exercise, reflect, and meditate, or choose not to. We can pick what to eat, how much to eat, when and with whom. We can even choose what to think, how to feel, what to see and what to hear. We can choose to appreciate and celebrate life. We can choose our associates, hobbies, and what skills we develop. We can select what type of music to listen to, movies to watch and books to read. Most importantly, we can choose what to believe and what to accept as true and whether or not to listen to *The Voice Within*,

To make the most of our freedom of choice, we must continuously educate ourselves, learn from our mistakes, detach, evaluate and weigh "costs vs. benefits" before we act. We have a mind to reason with, a heart to know by, and *The Voice Within* to guide us. To stand out and be an individual, we must first learn to use our freedom of choice.

The parable of the Prodigal Son is a parable about freedom of choice. The younger son chose to take his inheritance, leave his home, and be on his own. After squandering all of his wealth, he chose to return to his parents' home. Meanwhile, the older son elected to stay home with his parents. It is of the utmost importance to realize that in both cases they each used their freedom of choice and there was absolutely no judgment from the father. When the younger son returned home broke, the father welcomed him with open arms, put a ring on his finger and a robe over his shoulders. He ordered the fatted calf to be slaughtered in preparation for a feast celebrating his son's return. When the older son complained, the father made it crystal clear that he, meaning the older son, also had total freedom to do as he pleased. Having freedom of choice means that we can choose to live the way we please. There is no judgment. There are, however, consequences to all that we choose to do.

As we live, we are either doing our will or the will of someone else. Our will is on two levels. One is associated with our ego, survival and normal living and the other, a higher will, that of the Higher Self, is reserved for critical junctures in our lives. Whether we exercise our will, or the will of others, we are ultimately responsible for the consequences that follow. We can listen to the suggestions of others and ask for guidance, but once we act, it becomes our will. We have to live with the consequences. We reap what we sow.

Here are some factors that influence our use of freedom of choice:

Fear of Punishment or
Expectation of a Reward

A lot is made out of what Adam and Eve did in the Garden of Eden. They were told not to eat of a certain tree, but they did anyway. For that they were punished for all eternity. Whether or not Adam and Eve existed is irrelevant, but the story and their choice is. They were told they would die if they ate of the fruit of the tree. They ate anyway because the rewards of the opening of their eyes, knowing good from evil, and becoming like God were more powerful than their fear of death. For this, I applaud them. They exercised freedom of choice. Now they must face the consequences.

Fear of punishment or the expectation of a reward are powerful determinants in decision-making. However, merely deciding, out of fear or because of a reward without considering all options, is not intelligent. It does not reflect the use of an unbiased, freedom of choice.

Habit

Choosing out of habit is not exercising freedom of choice. Habits are a double-edged sword. On the one hand, they simplify our living and automate many functions that serve us. On the other hand, they eliminate thinking and true choice. Some activities, however, require thinking, decision-making and the use of our will. Living with awareness enhances our ability to use our freedom of choice.

Peer Pressure

We are social creatures. We want to be liked, accepted, and to fit in. Often, peer pressure plays a major role in decision-making. We are expected to act in a certain way, based on our religion, the influence of our parents, and obedience to authority. Complying with outside expectations when it does not reflect our deepest intentions is not exercising freedom of choice and is not a true choice. Cultivating high self-esteem and valuing our individuality are excellent countermeasures to peer pressure, as is exercising our will to make our own decisions.

Reason

Reasoned analysis constitutes thinking and sound decision-making. Reasoning involves looking at the whole, comparing pros and cons, checking costs/

benefits and then deciding. Reasoning is exercising freedom of choice. Reasoning and introspection are two pillars of intelligence.

Environment, Belief, Customs, Traditions

Succumbing to external factors, such as culture and history, is following the path of least resistance. This is a path laid out for us by others and is not an exercise of freedom of choice. Our environment, beliefs, customs and traditions have a lot to offer that enhance our lives. They can also act as a comfort zone that limits and traps us in a mediocre existence. These must be examined. Freedom of choice must be exercised in deciding what to accept and what to reject.

Knowing

Knowing goes beyond reasoning, logic, or any other factor. It is an inner feeling that is all-encompassing. It comes from deep within, from our Higher Self. When it does, we simply know what we need to do. When we know, we do not choose. We give in to the knowledge, and we act. Living based on knowing is the best way to live. It is the fastest route to growth and the expansion of consciousness. This requires that we remain in touch with *The Voice Within* and listen to its promptings.

Knowing is rare. It is usually associated with major life events. However, when it happens, it is crystal clear, self-evident, and unopposed. Some of the important circumstances that we need to know are choosing the right spouse to marry, deciding whether to have children, choosing a career, and settling on where to live. These require knowing.

When we find what we have been searching for, we know it instantly. We stop searching. Similarly, when faced with a choice and suddenly we know what to do, we must never hesitate. We must boldly act.

Nature, Instinct and Will

There is a major difference between freedom of choice and instinct. While instinct comes from nature, freedom of choice is a product of consciousness. Nature has instilled a variety of instincts in us, the purpose of which is survival and the propagation of the species. Nature does not "care" about individuals, only the species. Natural selection and survival of the fittest (to propagate the species) are natural forces. Improving the quality of our lives requires purposeful action. It involves using our freedom of choice. Nature will take care of the species. We must assume responsibility for our lives. For example:

1. Physically, we mature early. We are driven by nature through our hormones to mate. Our instinctual drive is to mate often and even with multiple partners. We can have sex at an early age and pregnancy can ensue.

Nature "cares" less whether or not we are emotionally, mentally and financially ready for a family. That responsibility is totally ours. We must prevent unwanted pregnancies, the transmission of disease, and the emotional damage that can result. We must use our freedom of choice to choose love over lust and to act responsibly.

2. The instinct to survive impels us to choose immediate gratification at the expense of our long-term benefit. We overeat, become addicted, and overspend because it feels good now. Instead, we should use our freedom of choice to plan our meals and eat in moderation, avoid addictive stimulation, and save for our future.

3. We are ingrained with fight or flight. We are wired with an instinct to compete, be selfish, and to react. We instinctively react to fire and loud noises. These help us to survive. Yet, through calculated action and willpower, we can go against our instincts. We can negotiate, cooperate, practice philanthropy, and be kind and compassionate.

4. To be social is instinctual. Therefore, we seek acceptance, popularity and fame. We are easily swayed by our leaders. We often follow blindly. We assume that our political leaders want the best for us. We believe that our theologians have the answers. We think that specialists will solve all of our problems. Yet, we can belong and be different, listen and reason, and get in touch with our innate divinity without a middleman. We can educate ourselves to use specialists to improve

our lives, instead of completely abdicating our authority and decision making to others.

Freedom of choice is a transformative tool. We can set it aside and not use it, or we can use it to make a difference in our lives and the lives of the many.

HOW FREE AM I?

There is no easy walk to freedom anywhere, and many of us will have to pass through the valley of the shadow of death again and again before we reach the mountaintop of our desires.

— *Nelson Mandela*

While on a recent visit to Jerusalem, a street vendor asked me where I was from. I replied: United States. He said: no, no, where are you really from? Once more, I replied: United States. He was not satisfied. He kept insisting on knowing where I was really from.

We can never be free from our looks, skin color, accent and inherited physical features. I will always be from the Middle East, even though I only lived there for 24 years and have lived in the United States for at least double that. Some things we can never be free of. If this is all we have to worry about, then we are doing great. However, most of the chains that bind us are not physical. Physical chains are obvious and can be broken. Mental, emotional, cultural and spiritual chains are much more difficult to detect and remove. They are not obvious, seldom acknowledged, and often accepted as an integral aspect of the self.

When I was a child in Syria, I believed that my country, religion, language and culture were the best. When I moved to Lebanon, I realized how limited my beliefs had been. I was born a Christian in the Middle East, indoctrinated with certain customs, traditions, and beliefs. Since these were all I knew, I adopted them as part of myself and they became my identity. I was shaped and molded by my circumstances. I did not question what I was taught by my elders and the authority figures in my life until I was much older. Whatever we learn and accept from our parents, teachers, and religions might limit and bind us. These were the best the past had to offer. They should be open to evaluation and enhancements.

We inherit a lot of things that facilitate how we live. These can also bind and restrict us. They define who we are and pit us against people that are not like us. We grow up believing that what is ours must be better than what is theirs. We send out missionaries to convert others to our way of living and believing, because what we have must be better than what they have. However, do we ever stop and question our own beliefs and whether or not what we are offering others is best for them? We believe that our "holy book" is the word of God, while theirs is not, for there can only be one book that is the word of God, the one we have. If what we believe is accurate, their beliefs must be false. Have we ever stopped and analyzed our beliefs first, before offering them to others? Growing up in Syria, I never questioned my beliefs. My questioning started while I was at the Monastery. Let us look at some of

what I was taught when I was young and impression-
able.

These are only five of thousands of beliefs I used to
have. Now let us take a closer look at these and shed
some light on them.

1. I Was Born In Sin And Require A Blood Sacrifice, That Of Christ, To Be Redeemed And Saved.

Nobody is ever born in sin unless sin is defined as
karma. We are born as a result of the sexual act, most to
a married couple, and as a result of love between two
individuals. Since both love and marriage are holy, we
are born holy.

Blood sacrifice is an ancient superstitious belief
that assumes a deity requires pacification or a bribe.
We must re-examine our beliefs regarding the one we
worship. Does it make sense that God, the creator of the
universe, wants or needs anything from any human?
We might believe otherwise, but that does not make
it true. God, the source of all, does not need anything
from any of His creations, especially blood sacrifices.

2. Christ Is The Only Son Of God.

Why is Christ the only son of God? Who are we,
if not the children of God? If God made us, we are God's
children just as Jesus is, or anyone else for that matter.
Beliefs are just that, beliefs, not facts. For many, Christ
was special, above all, the son of God. Christ was unique
in that he knew who he was – a son of God. Our problem
is that we are oblivious to who we are – children of God
as well. While Christ had high self-esteem, we lack it.
We do not believe that we can be special. Just because

we lack knowledge and self-esteem does not change the fact of who we are. We are just like Christ except in our knowledge and understanding. We have the same divine potential within. We can, and will eventually, attain Christhood.

3. Christ Was Born From Mary, The Virgin.

Why does Jesus have to be born from a virgin? Is it to fulfill an Old Testament prophecy? Was the word "virgin" accurately translated from its original Greek which referred to a young woman instead of a virgin? Is there anything wrong with a normal birth? Perhaps it was to indicate that his father was not an earthly being, just his mother. That makes Jesus a demigod. If Christ's father is not Joseph, how can he be from the house of David, since Joseph is a descendant of David, not Mary?

My intent is not to attack any religion. It is to question what we accept and believe. My purpose is to know, not to follow systems of thought or belief. I would much rather know than believe. Since beliefs, traditions, customs and any restrictive system of thought can limit our freedom, it behooves us to examine carefully what we accept and follow. To be free, we should be able to look at beliefs with an open mind, heart and spirit, objectively and dispassionately.

4. Christ Physically Rose From The Grave.

It is easy to believe that we are our bodies. The fact is that we are a soul currently residing in a body. Identifying with our physical bodies limits and restricts who we are, a living soul. Christ was not his body either. He was a living spirit not confined to his body.

There is no need to believe in a physical resurrection. It is not going to happen, for we are not our bodies. The fact is that we have had thousands of bodies over millennia of reincarnations. Even in the same lifetime, we experience a constantly changing body. Our bodies started as a single fertilized cell and have been changing ever since. Which body will be resurrected? Even though our cells are the ones building our bodies, we can, as consciousness, influence and direct their activities. In the final analysis, we are the architects of, not only our bodies, but of all our experiences as well.

Fear is a major factor that limits our ability to think clearly and then decide. Fear and ignorance keep us in the dark, accepting childish beliefs, refusing to question obvious contradictions, and going through life as if all is well. All is not well. Our humanity is at stake. Unless we are fearless, we cannot be free. I remember an incident in the monastery when I was a young student. We were in a Bible study class and my teacher was explaining how pleasing God leads to reward, while displeasing Him leads to punishment. The example he was using was from Exodus. God hardened the heart of the Pharaoh and he would not let the Israelites leave. Several punishments followed, one of which was the killing of the first-born children. I was appalled at the idea of killing innocent babies. I revolted and told my teacher that I could never worship a God who kills. The killing of innocent children is never acceptable under any circumstance. From that day on, I found my courage and became fearless. I believe that my fearlessness, over the years, was instrumental in setting me free - free to think, free to question, and free to appreciate what others have to offer.

I no longer defend my beliefs. I do not need to. I am always open to learning new things from any source. I appreciate, enjoy and celebrate what humanity has to offer. My diverse experiences have led me to know quite a lot over the years. There is still a lot I do not know and that is OK. As long as I live, I have time to find out, learn and improve.

5. My Language, Heritage And Culture Are Better Than Yours.

My language, heritage, and culture are not the best. They have some good features, so do other languages, cultures and heritages. We have no choice in where we are born, what language we grow up with and what foods we become accustomed to eating. We inherit, not only our parent's beliefs, but the culture of the country where we grow up. These are random. We cannot take credit for them. We are not favored with our circumstances. People in other countries inherit different languages, cultures and beliefs. None, intrinsically, is better or worse than others.

Having freedom of choice avails us the opportunity to learn any language, adopt any religion and adapt any culture to what we need to thrive. Everyone has something to contribute. What we consider "our language, cuisine, and culture", was the creation of the ones who preceded us. Perhaps, we can improve what we inherited before we pass them on to the next generation.

FREEDOM AND OUR HISTORY

The past is malleable and flexible, changing as our recollection interprets and re-explains what has happened.

— *Peter L. Berger*

After leaving the monastery in Zahle, Lebanon, I went to Sidon for high school. Since I hardly had any money, my missionary Aunt arranged for me to stay at a Christian Youth Hostel. We were all white, Christian, young males. One day, a new student joined us. He was from Uganda, Christian and black. Instantly, he was an outsider. No one wanted to befriend him. Very briefly, I had a similar reaction. However, I quickly overcame my initial aversion to our differences and befriended him.

What we believe, accept, and how we live is a reflection of the state of our mental and spiritual development. In other words, it is a gauge of our maturity. When humanity was young, it was acceptable to be superstitious, have primitive religions, and believe in magic. We were ignorant and needed help, so we were given prophets and laws. These were supposed to be temporary until we outgrew them. However, we held onto them as crutches that we could not survive without. Evolution is not only biological. Our consciousness must also evolve and, with it, our beliefs, laws, customs and traditions. Everything must evolve together. Christ came to get us out of our comfort zone and aid our growth. He was an example of the human potential. He showed us what we can be. He taught us that the literal interpretation of the law is not as important as understanding the spirit of the law. That is why He healed a man with a withered hand on the Sabbath. Christ was frustrated in His effort to nudge us into wakefulness. He described us as having eyes that cannot see; having ears that cannot hear and understand. (Matt 13:15).

Modern humans have replaced superstitions, magic and tribalism with unexamined beliefs, religious dogmas, and political convictions. These confine us to a tunnel vision that can be limited, biased and even discriminatory. We can have enlightened beliefs that uplift us. We can be religious and tolerant of others. We can belong to political parties if we learn to treat the opposition with respect and dignity. We can have status and be compassionate toward the less fortunate. We can be selective, but not be prejudiced. History can be used to propel us forward, if we learn from it. Our history has been one dominated by self-centeredness, wars and conquest. This warped history holds us hostage. We have to let go of anything that no longer serves us. We need to be objective, empathetic and compassionate instead of being right and feeling superior. Often, we forget what is most important. We place limiting beliefs ahead of what really matters. People are more important than beliefs, customs and traditions. Amicable relations are far better than hostilities. It takes courage to be open minded and free from bias. Freedom from our limiting beliefs is essential to creativity, innovation, and breakthroughs.

Freedom from my History

Where we are born and grow up shapes and molds us. Our culture gives us the necessities to live. It can also indoctrinate us to its nationalism, religion, language, customs, and history. How and where we grow up can have a lasting influence on us. Obviously, it is a double-edged sword with benefits and restrictions.

I spent my first few years in Aleppo, Syria. Then I moved to Lebanon and spent a few more years there. Finally, on February 14, 1972, I immigrated to the United States, after having received my permanent visa.

In Syria, I grew up in an abusive environment, very poor, and with hardly any modern conveniences. This molded my early consciousness. My early childhood introduced me to injustices that were difficult to cope with. I would wake up at night hearing the voice of my father waking up my mother to get him some water. I would think to myself: "Why wake up a sleeping person to get you water when you can easily get up and do it yourself?" The problem was that this was cultural. Women were not valued. I remember that even my brothers would ask my sister to do things for them that they could do themselves.

Syria is a patriarchy. Men are the head of the family. Their authority is unquestionable. Women are not as valuable as men. I learned that some tribes used to bury their females alive to avoid having them captured during a raid, to preserve their honor. Where is the honor in killing the female members of your family?

In Lebanon, women are respected and often treated equal to men. Lebanon has opposing political parties. People are cultured, free and open. Living in Lebanon broadened my outlook, especially during college. I was exposed to teachers, subjects and friends who were very different than what I had experienced before. I was fortunate to have an outspoken professor, Norman Frijerio, who had several graduate degrees, in addition to being a Catholic priest. He would hold open meetings where any subject was welcomed.

Living in the United States had the most impact on me. Basic training in the Army exposed me to people from many states. At Ft. Meade, I got to know highly talented and motivated people. Working at Walter Reed Army Medical Center and other U.S. Government agencies, and having taught for ten years vastly broadened my mind. Having cruised around the world, my consciousness is now infinitely different. I am a totally different person than when I was young. I do not claim the country of my birth as my nationality. My religious beliefs are vastly different than the ones I inherited. I no longer use my childhood language as a means of communication, or abide by the customs, traditions, or heritage of the Middle East. I have re-created myself. I choose what to accept, believe, adopt, and practice.

Yet, my early childhood still has a lingering influence upon me. I have mostly freed myself from the tentacles of my miserable early childhood. However, since I grew up lacking a great deal, I developed a poverty consciousness. Even though I now have sufficient means to obtain whatever I want or need, the influence of my early years lingers. I am still not fully free of my history. I still have work to do on myself. I have three specific areas I need to focus on:

1. Money

Since I barely had enough money to survive early on, that influence lingers in the recesses of my mind even though it is no longer relevant. I am generous in giving to others, but thrifty when spending on myself.

Money is an asset that must flow freely to have the greatest impact. If used properly, it can change lives. The loan I received from a caring lady for the first semester made all the difference in the quality of my life. Attending college and graduating transformed my future.

I must free myself of all hang-ups regarding money and find the most effective way to use money to make a difference, not only in my life, but in the lives of others as well.

2. Food

Since I did not have enough food when I was young, I tend to overcompensate now. Even though I am health conscious and selective about what I eat, I do not control the amount that I consume. Quality is under control, but the quantity not as much. I need to be more aware of the quantity and consume only what is required to maintain a healthy body.

3. Heritage

Middle Eastern people are stereotypically known for their generosity, hospitality and exaggerations. I admit to all of these. I am so used to exaggerations that I am seldom aware that I am exaggerating. Heritage, however, is not all cultural. My early upbringing had an even more lasting impact on my character. My wife loves to have fun. I am much more reserved. I am not as adventurous in trying out new activities. Since I was not exposed to fun activities while young, it is difficult for me to enjoy them now. That is why I do not swim much, rarely ski, and never play golf. I have a comfort zone for what activities I engage in. To be truly free, I cannot be confined or restrained when it comes to having fun. I must let loose and set myself free.

Examining my own history, I endeavor to use it to my advantage, instead of as a governing, limiting, and defining factor. Leaving my country of birth set me free to choose where to live. My constant study and lack of cultural influence enabled me to be free from constraining beliefs and dogmas. My knowledge and use of several languages also allowed me to communicate with different people and understand their unique points of view. My extensive travels, as well as my experiences living in several countries, exposed me to different cultures and a diverse set of people, beliefs, customs and traditions. It also helped to set me free from the belief that there is only one right way. There are numerous ways to live one's life, none of which is more or less correct than another. Living in a monastery, serving in the U.S. Army, and having lived in the Middle East and the United States have all helped to broaden my perspective. My diverse careers in medicine, information systems and education also broadened my mind and contributed toward my gaining freedom to pursue more than one vocation. I am now a citizen of the world. I welcome diversity and am able to live in peace with anyone, anywhere in the world.

I value cooperation and genuine human relations. I am not only tolerant, but aware, of the benefits of diversity. I am open and free. I constantly strive to learn, discover and improve. I will never cease to continue to shed the scales of ignorance. I seek to be understanding and compassionate. Above all, my motto is coexistence, acceptance and better relations with others.

A GARDEN ON EARTH

No occupation is so delightful to me as the culture of the earth, and no culture comparable to that of the garden.

— *Thomas Jefferson*

Earth is a marvel to behold. It is beautiful, multi-faceted, and diverse. It has gardens, deserts, mountains, valleys, rivers, lakes and oceans. Earth can easily be referred to as the proverbial Eden.

There is a garden in this Eden and it is humanity. Not everyone's life is a garden. This is because of freedom of choice and the level of consciousness of each human. Regardless of where we live, we can create our own garden. To do this requires us to assume our role as gardeners and take thoughtful action.

A garden is an intricate balance, requiring constant care and maintenance, just like our lives. A garden has soil in which we can drop seeds. Humans have a subconscious that acts as fertile soil. The Garden of Eden had an Adam, an Eve, two main trees, a serpent, four rivers and a God. Humans have an Adam, the male human and an Eve, the female human. They also have two trees: the tree of knowledge - the brain, spinal cord, and the nervous system, and the tree of life - the heart and the circulatory systems. The serpent is that which tempts. The serpent in our garden is our thoughts, desires, hopes and aspirations. These lead to action. The four rivers are our habits, attitudes, expectations and beliefs. These direct our energies along established paths.

We also have a God in our garden. It is our Higher Self, the aspect of divinity that resides within our soul. It speaks to us through *The Voice Within*. The story tells us that God told Adam, **not Eve**, not to eat of the Tree of Knowing Good and Evil. The serpent tempted **Eve**. Eve succumbed and convinced Adam to eat of the fruit as well. God was angry at being disobeyed and punished both Adam and Eve by expelling them from the garden.

Since this story employs a talking serpent, I classify it as a fable. Fables are not meant to be literal. They are symbolic and convey a lesson to be learned, a moral to be embraced. Fables can be interpreted in different ways.

Here is what I think is the hidden meaning and the moral of this story:

1. We have freedom of choice

2. There are consequences to all choices and actions. Some choices lead to "paradise and heaven" while other choices lead to "earth, struggle and hell". Most consequences are somewhere in between.

3. The result of choice is experience – the opening of the eyes - and eventual knowledge.

4. There is no immediate death as a result of our choices, only consequences and learning.

5. We are "tempted" or persuaded by an appeal to our feminine aspect (Eve), the heart and emotions, instead of the male aspect (Adam), the mind and reasoning.

In heaven, God is the owner of the garden. On earth, the human is the owner of the garden, in the sense that our lives are ours to do with as we please. We are responsible for the results we reap. In the end, whether we end up in heaven or in hell depends upon our actions and the choices we make. We can listen to our selfish thoughts and give in to desire and temptation, or we can be guided by our Higher Self and live with intention and integrity, in the service of spiritual growth.

Finally, it is through experience that our eyes open, that we wake up, learn and make better decisions. The more diverse our experiences, the stronger our root system becomes and the faster we grow and mature. For to live is to experience and create memories. To remember is to learn, to grow and to mature. To mature is the ultimate purpose of living.

Earth is Eden and we live in this Eden. We choose whether we live in a garden, a desert, or somewhere in between. We are the caretakers. If we assume responsibility for our lives, we can transform our lives into beautiful gardens. If we do not and are careless, the gardens of our lives will atrophy and slowly turn into deserts.

MY LIFE AS A GARDEN

It is the lives we encounter that make life worth living.

— *Guy de Maupassant*

My life has been a garden, a desert and everything in between. Even though I like to experience variety, I mostly prefer my life to be a garden. A garden is created and maintained intentionally. To maximize the number of fragrant, full-blooming flowers and fruit trees, I must be a good gardener: guarding, weeding and feeding, on an ongoing basis.

My garden is the result of the seeds that were planted there. Some seeds were planted subconsciously, due to culture and environment, a few by necessity, and a handful intentionally. While some seeds have germinated and are growing nicely, others remain dormant, awaiting the opportunity to sprout and begin to grow. A few have grown into majestic trees, bearing wonderful fruit, while others remain barren and simply occupy space.

My garden has three main trees in it. Two are visible and well-known, while the third is invisible and, in many ways, feeble and stunted. The first is the tree of life and represents my heart, with its circulatory system; the second is the tree of knowing, reasoning, and understanding and represents my mind, brain and nervous system; while the third tree is my inspiration, intuition and *The Voice Within*.

The tree of life is the tree of living and experiencing. As we live and experience, we learn, grow, and mature; our eyes open, we awaken, and the quality of our life improves. The tree of knowing, the mind, must be cultivated through continued education. As we accumulate knowledge, we awaken and we get to know. Thus, these two trees, heart and mind, are eternally intertwined, and influencing each other. I also seek inspiration, listen to my intuition and follow the guidance of *The Voice Within*.

My heart, mind, inspiration and intuition must be used together. Reason without compassion is lifeless and compassion without reason enables dependence. After using my mind and consulting my heart, I allow for inspiration, intuition and *The Voice Within* to spring forth and guide my decisions.

There are also four rivers that course through my garden, feeding, nurturing and stimulating it. These rivers must flow to purify and remove any debris that might block the flow of the life force within me. Stagnant rivers are a breeding ground for germs and disease.

The first river is the most powerful and sets the course for the others. My habits represent this river. Habits form intentionally or accidentally, as a result of repetition. Helpful, intentional habits are our best servants. Forming useful habits, my garden will be well cared for, easier to maintain, and will continue to blossom and bear fruit.

My attitudes equate to the second river in the garden of my life. Attitudes steer my life and are responsible for a major portion of my accomplishments. My attitudes affect my endocrine glands that control the functioning of my body. I endeavor to maintain a positive mental attitude.

My expectations symbolize the third river in the garden of my life. We conduct ourselves based upon the expectations we have of others and ourselves. Whatever we expect, with confidence, becomes our self-fulfilling prophecy. Expectations fine-tune our receptors and are like antenna, eager to catch that which we expect. We can expect a lot from ourselves and others, however, we must guard against that, for we can easily be disappointed.

My beliefs embody the fourth river in the garden of my life. Like the aperture of a camera, my beliefs are the windows through which I see the world. Beliefs are a collection of mental structures that organize and hold our thoughts, feelings, perceptions, and memories in place. Beliefs influence all of our experiences. Ultimately, how we perform depends on our beliefs, which inform our worldviews. I periodically examine my beliefs. I nurture the empowering ones and root out the debilitating ones.

Starting a garden is labor intensive. In its early stages, a garden requires more care. Pain and suffering anchor my roots in the soil of my subconscious. Pleasure and joy extend my branches to touch the heavens. A tree, by nature, is always dynamically involved in its environment. Its roots dig deep into the soil, absorbing water and nutrients, while its limbs extend upward toward the heavens, welcoming wind and the rays of sunlight. Therefore, in order to grow, I must be like the tree. I must be involved in all aspects of life, using what I encounter and experience as an opportunity to learn, to discover and to improve. As I learn and mature, the scales of ignorance covering my eyes will gradually fall off. I will see clearly and I will know. As I know, my ignorant self will die and my light will shine, unobstructed.

A garden is a microcosm. Everything is interconnected in a garden, as it is on earth, and in my life. While these four rivers are essential to my garden, my garden also requires rain, wind and sunshine. Rain cleanses and hydrates me. Wind and storms blow away the old, the debris, and prune and strengthen by removing the dead branches. Sunshine bathes me in merriment, laughter, joy, warmth and beauty.

Plants in a garden are involved in the soil and their environment, which is clearly evident in their root systems. My life should reflect this in my engagements and relations with others. The deeper and the more intimate the involvement of the root system with the soil, the better, healthier, and stronger the fruit and fragrance of my garden. So it is with my engagements and relationships.

I am a constant gardener, continuously dropping deliberate seeds and caring for them. At the same time, I tirelessly remove undesirable weeds. My life is a metaphoric garden that I can take with me wherever I go. I would like this garden to be a temple of beauty, harmony and peace. I can visit it whenever I like to let go of my worries, concerns and burdens. I can also infuse my being with its intoxicating fragrance and rejuvenating vitality.

OBEY OR DISOBEY

All I've done all my life is disobey.

— Edith Piaf

Quite often, my Dad's frustrations with his lot in life translated into brutality. Once when I came home from elementary school, he asked me where I was.

"In school," I answered.

"No, you were not," he said, "Tell me the truth."

"I am telling the truth. I was in school. You can verify it by checking with the school and my teachers."

He said: "I do not need to check with the school. I want you to tell me the truth."

"But that is the truth. I was in school like I always am."

My dad grabbed my hand and pulled me toward him. He shoved the door open and dragged me through the street to a lady's house that I had never seen. He knocked on the door. A lady opened the door, looked at me, then at my Dad and said: "Yes, that's him. That is the boy who threw a rock and broke my window." My Dad began to punch and kick me. He did not stop even after we got home. He ordered everyone out, locked the door and began to whip and punch me. He insisted that I should admit that, I, in fact, broke the window. Since I did not do such a thing. I refused to obey.

The beatings continued unmercifully for a long time. My mother was pleading with me from outside, to confess so the beatings would stop. I refused. Eventually, I realized that this would not end until I lied. So, I did. I was brutalized more often than I care to remember, all for refusing to obey my Dad, to tell a lie or to give him false information. We are encouraged to respect, honor and obey our parents. What if they never earn it or deserve it?

According to Judeo-Christian and Islamic traditions, the first humans were placed in a garden and given the choice to obey or disobey a command by God to not eat from a certain tree. We are led to believe that we can only choose to exercise our freedom of choice one way – the way that pleases God. We are also told that we must obey God's commandments. If we don't, we will be punished.

Let us examine this premise. Does it make sense that we should be given an option that is really not an option at all? Does it make sense that God would test us with a tempting fruit tree by placing it in the middle of the garden? Does God command humans? To what end? Does God require obedience or anything from humans? Do our stories, or more accurately fables, make sense?

Let us take a closer look at another of these commandments:

You shall not kill.   *Exodus 20:13.*

Does this commandment apply in all cases? Why, then, do we go to war and kill? How about in self-defense? Does this commandment exclude the killing of animals? How do we know that? If killing is forbidden, why did the angels of the Lord kill the first born of the Egyptians? How about the murder of 185,000 Assyrian soldiers?

> And that night the angel of the LORD went out and struck down 185,000 in the camp of the Assyrians. And when people arose early in the morning, behold, these were all dead bodies.
>
> 2 Kgs 19:35

How about trying to extinguish all life from Earth through a flood?

> For behold, I will bring a flood of waters upon the earth to destroy all flesh in which is the breath of life under heaven. Everything that is on the earth shall die.
>
> Gen 6:17

God is not a person with human qualities. According to Christ, no one has ever seen or can see God, for God is a "spirit."

> God is spirit, and those who worship him must worship in spirit and truth. John 4:24
>
> No one has ever seen God; if we love one another,

God abides in us and his love is perfected in us. 1 John 4:12

No one has ever seen God; the only God, who is at the Father's side, he has made him known. John 1:18

God is never seen, and does not command or tempt. Only humans do that. Likewise, only humans reward or punish. It is humans who instill fear in us as a means of control. God has no reason to command us, instill fear in us, or punish us. God only loves us. Nothing is from God unless it is love. Love neither commands nor controls.

I learned long ago to let go of my fear. In every situation, I consult my God given-gifts: reason, conscience, and *The Voice Within* before I accept or reject a belief system. I obey or disobey based on my logic, common sense, and how I feel within. To live in fear of punishment is the opposite of living a free and unencumbered life. I fearlessly take full responsibility for my beliefs and for my decisions to obey or disobey.

Our society is hierarchical. We have bosses, officials, and authority figures. Often, we are asked or ordered to do something, nevertheless we have a choice to obey or disobey. As children, in general, we should obey our parents, for they know better and have our best interests at heart. As patients, we should obey our physicians, for they know better and have our welfare in mind. Obeying experts who know better is wise. However, as we become mature adults, we must evaluate every situation and decide for ourselves.

Freedom of choice is a gift that comes with re-sponsibilities. It is through our choices, right or wrong, that we learn, grow, and mature. There are no right or wrong choices, but there are consequences. The consequences of our actions are our reward or punishment. The story of the Prodigal Son clearly demonstrates the absence of judgment. The Father couldn't wait to welcome his son with open arms, cover him with the best robe, and adorn him with a ring. There was no judgment whatsoever, regardless of what the son had done.

But the father said to his servants, 'Bring quickly the best robe, and put it on him, and put a ring on his hand, and shoes on his feet. And bring the fattened calf and kill it, and let us eat and celebrate. For this my son was dead, and is alive again; he was lost and is found. And they began to celebrate.'   *Luke 22-24*

We are on earth to exercise our gift of freedom of choice and through the consequences of our choices, we learn, grow, and mature. Over time, we make better decisions and become more effective. We are responsible for our choices. We can intentionally direct the course of our lives and shape our destiny, or we can live in fear of consequences and become paralyzed. We are individual, unique and valuable, but only if we recognize our gift of choice and exercise our right to choose wisely and decide who and what to obey, or willfully disobey.

AM I MY BROTHER'S KEEPER?

If we are not our brother's keeper, at least let us not be his executioner.

—*Marlon Brando*

We are born into a spectacular world – Earth with all of its beauty and splendor. Are we here merely to have fun, enjoy ourselves, and be happy and live for as long as we can? Or do we have responsibilities and obligations as well?

Nature is balanced and harmonious. There is give and take, push and pull. Everything is seemingly coupled with an opposite or a complement. There is day and night, cold and hot, male and female, attraction and repulsion, growth and decay, life and death. Freedom is also coupled with responsibility. Because of our freedom of choice, we can choose to ignore our responsibilities. However, we are all connected, links in the chain of humanity. We inhabit one earth, breathe the same air, and depend upon one another. What we do matters. We cannot take without giving back. It upsets the laws of balance and reciprocity. Therefore, it makes sense that we have responsibilities and obligations.

Even though our responsibilities might be clear, oftentimes our obligations are not. We are responsible for our decisions and our actions. We are also responsible for what we do with our time, resources, skills and abilities. We are responsible for what we think and how we feel. Additionally, we are responsible for what we produce and create. We are especially responsible for those we bring into this world, our children. How responsible we are depends on our level of awareness and the acceptance of our responsibilities. Obligations are different from responsibilities. They are more abstract. Some feel an obligation to their culture and history. Others feel an obligation to follow their parents' career or religion, speak a certain language, or follow specific customs or traditions. I, on the other hand, choose to embrace only three obligations:

First, I am obligated to truth, wherever and whenever I encounter it. I listen to *The Voice Within* and follow the dictates of my conscience as freely as I can without any fear of repercussions. I am not on earth to live for systems or to defend their existence. I am here to learn from all sources, to shine my light, and to proclaim my personal truth.

Second, I have an obligation to earth and the environment. While Earth is my home, the environment is my lifeline. My survival depends on it.

Third, I also have an obligation to be my brother's keeper. Over the years, I have received assistance that made a difference in my life. Only with assistance was I able to transition from need to sufficiency and from receiving to giving. I have an obligation to lend a helping hand whenever I can. I do so with respect, dignity, and with the intention to empower.

I am my brother's keeper because others took care of me when I needed help. Now it is my turn. By recognizing the cycles of life, its ups and downs, we all benefit by being each other's keepers. Each of us is a cell in the body that is humanity. Caring only for ourselves leads us to a selfish, cancerous existence. Caring for each other leads us to health and vibrancy. It is an easy choice to make. Interdependence makes us all each other's keepers. Additionally, our happiness comes from genuinely assisting others. We are all one big, interconnected family. We rise together and we fall together. We are one and the same, merely at different stages of development.

PRIVILEGE

Life is a gift, and it offers us the privilege, opportunity, and responsibility to give something back by becoming more. — *Tony Robbins*

Whil e touring Mumbai, India it was obvious that there are two classes of people living there: the very poor and the very wealthy. Our Indian tour guide pointed to a building and said, "That building over there, worth $40 million U.S. dollars, was given by a father to his daughter as a wedding gift." I immediately thought, "How fortunate for the daughter and her husband." Why would she be so privileged, while so many others are underprivileged? Is there a system or a law that determines privilege or is it random and capricious? If a child is born to poor parents, is that by law, by choice, or is it simply the luck of the draw? And if another child is born to wealthy parents, is that too by law, by choice, or simply luck?

How could there be justice if neither child did anything to earn the circumstances into which they were born? If things happen randomly, and children are born to parents regardless of merit, or choice, then there can never be justice and God cannot exist, or God does not care and is uninvolved in the human condition. Favoritism cannot be part of God's nature, for we are all God's children.

How can we explain such disparities?

We know laws govern nature. We study these laws in school. Plants and animals are also governed by natural laws. People are part of nature as well. Do laws also govern human affairs, albeit a different set of laws, perhaps spiritual laws, that take freedom of choice and its consequences into consideration? I believe so.

If humans did not experience the consequences of their actions, then there could be no justice. I believe that justice is always served, albeit over several lifetimes. Life is not senseless, random, or blind. I know life to be orderly, purposeful, and responsive to consciousness. Life is never capricious. Life is an education system in which we learn valuable lessons. The object of living is neither punishment nor reward. It is learning, growing and maturing.

We grow as a result of experience. We attract the conditions we need in order to gain mastery of situations. Once we master one circumstance, we move on to the next. We are governed by spiritual laws that make life fair for everyone. Two such laws are karma and reincarnation. Karma provides us with consequences for our actions, while reincarnation guarantees justice, over long periods of time.

Life is beautiful because it makes sense. We experience the consequences of our actions by living many lives until justice is served and lessons are learned. That gives our lives its ups and downs, which make our lives less predictable. By employing our freedom of choice and by constantly learning and improving our skills, we can change our fate. We can move from deficiency to sufficiency or even abundance. We can progress from privation to privilege; however, with privilege comes responsibility.

God or nature does not favor the child born to wealthy parents. Equally, the child born to destitute parents is not being punished. It is not where we start in life that is important; it is where we finish. Both children have freedom of choice. Both have the opportunity to grow and blossom. The rich child has more responsibilities because more has been given to him or her. The poor child must use his or her freedom of choice and make the appropriate choices, to overcome challenges and progress. Environments are malleable. What we do with them is up to us. By pursuing education and continuous learning, by developing skills and abilities, and by excelling, the poor and underprivileged can put themselves on the fastest and surest path to create the life they desire. Similarly, the wealthy can use their wealth responsibly to affect the most good. Since we live many lives, the poor of one lifetime may be the rich in the next and vice versa. Everything balances out in the long run.

Experiences are what we need to grow. Often these experiences are the result of previous causes, or karma, from previous lifetimes. All actions, whether conscious or not, result in consequences. These can be favorable or challenging. We can take specific actions to bring about the results we want. We can transform challenges into opportunities. Life is just because we live many lives and, through freedom of choice and conscious intent, we can create our fortunes or misfortunes. Wealth and poverty are opportunities for action. Privilege, on the other hand, is a responsibility.

THE TRANSIENT AND
THE ENDURING

*For this light momentary affliction is preparing
for us an eternal weight of glory beyond all com-
parison, as we look not to the things that are seen
but to the things that are unseen. For the things
that are seen are transient, but the things that
are unseen are eternal.*   — *2 Cor 4:17-18*

O h how time flies and with it, our lives. When I
was in elementary school, we had a celebration. Several students were assigned to participate and I was one of them. My role was to read the following passage from the Bible:

*Do not lay up for yourselves treasures on earth,
where moth and rust destroy and where thieves
break in and steal, but lay up for yourselves
treasures in heaven, where neither moth nor
rust destroys and where thieves do not break in
and steal. For where your treasure is, there your
heart will be also.   Matt 6:19-21*

I never forgot this passage. It stuck with me.
When I became an adult, I learned the 80/20 percent

rule. 80% of all that we undertake or experience is trivial and transient, while 20% is relevant with lasting impact. I learned to focus on the critical few tasks and ignore the rest. This is analogous to what Christ admonished us to do: to seek treasures that do not spoil, where rust and moth have no power. In other words, seek the critical things that are important and that endure.

Earth is the domicile of the senses and the transient, while heaven eludes the senses and is host to the enduring. The treasures of heaven that do not spoil are the lives we touch and are touched by, the loving service we render, the memories we create, the lessons we learn, the character we build, and the knowledge we attain. All the rest are faux treasures of earth. The foods we eat, the clothes we wear, the houses we live in, the cars we drive, and the funds we accumulate, are transient. While the faux treasures of earth are seen and are subject to the senses, the genuine treasures of heaven are metaphysical.

Another way to look at the transient and the enduring is to think of what we remember and what we forget. Canvassing our memories, what do we remember? Are these fond memories? Then we should endeavor to create similar memories in the lives of those we care about, especially our children. Are the memories sad and painful? Then we should do our best to prevent these from ever happening to others.

My wife and I just came back from a walk in the park. The park is beautiful with a large man-made lake. How much of this walk will I remember? For how long? Since we have walked this park hundreds of times, I will forget this walk in a day or two. If something un-usual had happened while we were walking, then the memory would last longer. Based on intensity, value and relevance, certain memories endure, while the vast majority are transient. The effects of traumas and certain emotionally charged incidents have an endur-ing influence upon us, some lasting a lifetime.

All of our experiences are fleeting, yet they are the gateways to the enduring and the permanent. The idea of experiencing permanent qualities, such as beauty and harmony, through the transient is reflected by the creation of special gardens in Japan and China. These gardens exude permanent qualities of harmony and tranquility through the artistic placement of tran-sient materials such as water, plants, and rocks.

The Japanese are well aware that it is through the transient that we can create the enduring, and through the imperfect that we can realize perfection. They reason that because nothing lasts and everything is transient, it becomes important to celebrate the temporary in a special way. The Japanese tea ceremony known as "Wabi Sabi" is a reflection of this philoso-phy. A tea-drinking ceremony is enacted to celebrate the transient. The setting reflects the imperfect nature of the material world and its transiency, yet the cere-mony endows endurance to the transient. Even though the tea ceremony uses imperfect accouterments, the setting is a reflection of harmony, respect, purity and tranquility. These are ideals and are permanent.

We can seek the enduring, but we can never grasp it and hold onto it. The best we can do is create it and let it go. If we live exemplary lives, guided by ideals, such as justice, compassion and love, then we are creating that which endures. What endures is not the same as what is permanent. Absolute permanence is not desirable because it perpetuates the status quo and makes improvements impossible. Lasting impact is what we want.

Our lives are fleeting and transient. Our days are numbered, and that is what makes life precious. Let us not waste our lives seeking the transient. Instead, let us seek the treasures that do not spoil. Our resources are time, money, skills and goods. We can use these for trivia, or we can use them to create enduring memories. We can give our children temporary gratification or we can give them memories that last a lifetime. The best use of our time is to leave lasting impacts in the lives of others. Personally, we can use our time to educate ourselves and to cultivate important skills such as mastering the art of relationships. An excellent use of our resources is to travel and experience diverse cultures. The treasures that do not spoil are at hand if only we know where to look and what to seek.

The most valuable treasure that never spoils is love. Let us make our hearts the abode of this one emotion – love – a treasure of heaven that endures forever.

JOURNEY TO ENOUGH

He who knows that enough is enough will always have enough.

— *Lao Tzu*

The lowest point in my life was the summer of 1967. Because of the 6-day war, I could not get a job. The only person who could have helped was a woman we knew in Aleppo whom my mother had worked for as a cleaning lady. She was an American Presbyterian missionary who we called Aunt Faith. Foreigners evacuated Beirut because of the war and my Aunt had to leave. Before she departed, she left money with a friend to take care of her cat Cleo. She left nothing for us. With no job or family support, I was in survival mode. I had to pawn my belongings to pay for absolute necessities. I learned to survive on 25 cents a day. Those days are far behind me now.

When we came to the U.S., my family took two different paths. Having come from a background of not having enough, some of us overcompensated and spent money they did not have. The rest of us became conservative in our ways, spending less and saving for a rainy day, remembering what it was like to not have enough.

It is easy to lose sight of what is important when we are surrounded by plenty. However, it is deprivation that teaches us value. Abject poverty teaches some people appreciation for what is important, while others take a different path, a path to greed, wanting more and more. Greed is defined as: "an uncontrolled longing for increase in the acquisition or use: of material gain (be it food, money, land, or animate/inanimate possessions); or social value, such as status, or power." (Wikipedia). It is absolutely fine to seek what we need. The problem arises when we do not know when to stop. That is why greed is one of the seven deadly sins. It has no boundaries. Boundaries are essential.

Our experiences revolve around two aspects: the bound and limited and the boundless and limitless. In the human, the body is the bound, while the boundless is the soul with its attributes of consciousness, imagination and creativity. Incidentally, the ancients referred to the bound as earth and to the boundless as heaven. I have learned a great deal just by observing and studying the human body. I am amazed as to how the body knows when to stop growing. The toes "know" exactly how far to extend. So do the arms, legs, lungs and heart. It would be a major problem if the body did not know when to stop growing. The body is an incredibly successful organism. We can emulate the body in many ways.

What is of the material earth is the limited and transient. What is of the immaterial heaven is the boundless and eternal. It is easy to confuse the two. Unhappiness results when we do not know one from the other. We need just enough of the material to enjoy our earthly experiences. There is no limit to how much of the heavenly we can accrue. The treasures of heaven are limitless, real, lasting and do not spoil. Once obtained, no thief can take them away from us. They can never be lost. These are incorporated in us as an aspect of our soul manifesting as personality. These treasures are carried within us from one lifetime to the next.

Taking a closer look at our material and earthly possessions, we find boundaries everywhere. What is a house but bound space, with limits? What is a shirt, pants, or a spoon but examples of bound material? Material things must be defined and limited, with boundaries. Countries have borders that are defined and limited. Cars have boundaries. An hour is measured and limited. A school year is defined and numbered. The clothes and the shoes we wear are bound and must fit. Games start and end. I was on a cruise ship that circumnavigated the Earth. It took us 120 days to complete this journey around the globe. One time, we went 10 days and nights non-stop without seeing any land. Even though the oceans are immense, they are still limited. Everything on earth is limited by boundaries, except for outer space, which is immaterial. Therefore, let our wants, needs and desires for the material be defined, limited, and tailored to fit our needs. The material journey of life is the journey to have enough. It is a journey to satisfy needs. The spiritual journey of life is a journey of manifesting our divine potential. It is the journey of continuous growth to maturity that can be approached, but never fully attained.

What is enough varies from person to person. Regardless, we should never seek more than what we can use. Once we have enough food to nourish the body and comforts to enjoy life, then that is enough. Once we have enough clothes, shoes, living space for our well-being, then that is enough. Once we have enough money to live contentedly and enjoy life, then that is enough. Each person can decide how much 'material' they need. If we do not have boundaries and we always want more and more, we will never be content and it will be difficult to be happy. Greed and its companion fear are often the most important factors as to why people buy or sell stocks. With greed, we can easily be exploited. Greed is insatiable; it is continuously seeking, without boundaries or limits. Ambition, on the other hand, is the desire to improve one's quality of life. It is normal and desirable. Unlike greed, that is boundless, ambition has boundaries. Happiness comes from the attainment of objectives and the realization of goals. If there is no limit to what we want, how can we ever achieve contentment, and be happy?

We can determine what is enough for us and go after it. We can seek it until we attain it. Once we do, we can settle back and enjoy our achievement. There is only one justifiable reason to want more. It is in order to give to others. That is a noble cause. Once we have enough of the material, we can seek the boundless immaterial. We can seek knowledge, wisdom and understanding. We can express compassion and practice forgiveness. We can use our imagination and creativity. We can exude ever-increasing love, appreciate more and more beauty, and experience ongoing joy. We can give back in loving service. These are of heaven and are boundless. These are the treasures that do not spoil.

THE PATH LESS TRAVELLED

There are basically two types of people. People who accomplish things, and people who claim to have accomplished things. The first group is less crowded.

—*Mark Twain*

I had only been in the United States for five months when I joined the Army. Basic training at Ft. Dix, N.J. was not easy. It was more manageable for me than others who had heard how difficult it would be. I had no clue what to expect. What was surprising to me was what the recruits did on breaks. They would rush to the Commissary, get a 6-pack of beer, and sit outside on the grass and drink. I chose differently: reading, writing and improving my command of the English language. We all make choices, neither good nor bad, just with different consequences, especially over the long haul.

There are two paths in life: the wide, well-paved path that is used by the masses and the narrow, uncharted path that is walked by the few. The masses are followers. The few are innovators, creators, and leaders who venture forth fearlessly and chart their own course.

While young and dependent, we follow our parents. As adults, however, we need to examine our lives and, if needed, chart our own course. We can do this intelligently and without unnecessary confrontation.

It is easy to fall in line, to be one of many, to want to be liked and accepted. We mostly live shallow lives, going along, not making waves, taking the path most travelled. This is fine for the many, but not for those individuals born to make a difference in their own lives and the lives of the many. These people embody the spirit of individualism and clearly understand the gift of freedom of choice. They know that improving their lives does not happen on its own. If something needs to get done, then it is up to **them** to do it. For these individuals, personal freedom is always balanced by an equal sense of responsibility to themselves, their community and to humanity.

It is acceptable to follow if our actions are based on understanding, and if our conscience is at peace. We do not have to choose between being a standout individual or a member of the collective, for we can be both. We can follow when following does not compromise our principles. We can be a standout when we can make a positive contribution.

Following is easy. We can do it with our eyes closed. It is more demanding to be awake and live consciously. There is a major difference between those who sleepwalk through life and those who are awake. Awakened or enlightened people, exercise freedom of choice and act with intent and responsibility. They are the difference makers.

We are asleep if we simply follow and never question what we are doing and why. We are awake if we take charge and direct our own course in life. Following others requires giving up our responsibility to leaders, organizations, and institutions, and simply letting them decide for us. This can simplify our lives, but it can also be dangerous. Institutions can be sincere but narrow-minded. They can also be fanatical in the defense of their way. They can be judgmental of others. They can twist the truth to meet their needs. They can also be controlling and complicit to injustice. If we simply follow without questioning, we silence our conscience and are complicit.

We are both individual and social. We do not live alone or only for ourselves. Sometimes we can follow, while other times we must choose a separate path, our own. Society creates opportunities for individuals. It is the individual, however, who advances society. Growth comes from effort. The more effort we put into living our unique lives, the faster we will grow and mature. Additionally, being an individual does not preclude us from working with others who share a similar philosophy. In fact, it is best to find individuals and organizations that reflect our philosophy of life, and work together to achieve common goals. The path less travelled does not have to be lonely and boring. There are many who share our philosophy of life. We can share our travels with them. It is more fun.

ENERGY, FORCE AND POWER

*The knowledge that we are responsible for living
the life we have is our most powerful tool.*

—*Srikumar Rao*

We are familiar with the three states in nature: solids, liquids and gases. Solids have defined volume and shape. Liquids have defined volume, but no defined shape. They can move. Gases have neither defined volume nor shape. Gases can disperse and soar. All three are energy and energy is of three types: random, directed and purposeful.

People are either in the random energy state, the directed energy state or the purposeful energy state. These states are not caste systems that keep people confined to one state. People have the freedom to move to the next state through specific steps that they can take. Regardless of where people are, everyone has the energy, the force and the power to think, to plan, and to achieve.

Random Energy State

When I was young, I was in the random energy state. I was in survival mode. I had energy like everyone else. However, this energy was "random", "diffused", "dispersed", and "formless". My actions were impulsive, and I functioned without any priority, aim, or purpose. A person who is unorganized or haphazard is in a random state of energy, in aimless motion. There is apparent activity, but little to show for it. There are two forms of energy: kinetic and potential. Kinetic energy is energy of movement, while potential energy is our energy reservoir. Potential energy can be actualized by tapping into our abundant reservoir. We do this by getting organized, setting goals, and by delving into what interests us.

We start life as "stem" organisms, undifferentiated and capable of learning and being anything. We are full of potential energy. This potential energy is very powerful due to the "Divine Potential" inherent in our genes. Initially, the difference between this potential and our realized self is vast. This propels us forward into a powerful wave of growth and development. As we accumulate experiences and grow into adulthood, we "specialize" and become set in our ways. The difference between our potential and actual energies diminishes, and with it the level of our energy, desire, and interest. We begin to atrophy. It is as if the "money" we started life with is slowly being spent. If we do not replenish this "money", we age and die.

We can replenish ourselves and move to the next level by adding direction and quality to our physical activity. We can also tap into our potential energy more frequently by adding new adventures into our lives. We can travel, learn new skills and develop new abilities. This requires that we maintain our interest and curiosity.

Directed Energy State

When I got married and my wife and I started a family, my life changed. My life was no longer random. My energy became focused and directed. My actions were thought out, planned, and motivated. I had to provide and care for my family. I graduated from being in the random energy state to the directed energy state. My energy transformed into force.

There are two forms of force: physical and mental. While physical force is directed energy, mental force is the result of establishing tracks in the brain for energy to flow through. These are the habits, attitudes, expectations, beliefs and knowledge we accumulate through living and experiencing.

What changes random energy into force is focus and direction. These can be provided by goals, intent, and a plan of action. These are vector energies, focused and directed. Goals are the future achievements we desire. It is the "**what**" of what we want. Intent is knowing "**why**" we want what we seek to achieve. Why is this goal important to attain? How will it make a difference in our lives? Many agree that if we are clear on the "**why**", then it is easy to devise a "**how**" to get there. A plan of action includes specific steps, with timeframes, as to how and when we intend to reach our goals. It directs our energy into specific channels or steps needed to achieve our goal.

Purposeful Energy State

When I finally approached maturity, my use of energy became "leveraged" and "impactful". I was no longer focused on myself, my family or my personal goals. I was comfortable with myself. My focus and intention moved to serving and empowering others. I wanted to make a difference in the lives of the many. I chose education as my new tool. I had a new type of energy: purposeful. Purposeful energy is power. It leads to achievement.

There are two forms of power: temporal and spiritual. Many seek temporal power, in one form or another. Some seek it through acquiring a fortune. Others wield power through position, status, or vested authority. Spiritual power is different. It involves enlightened consciousness manifesting as love, compassion, genuine care, and service. While temporal power is fickle, spiritual power is permanent. True and lasting spiritual power is our ultimate goal. It is the heaven we seek and the state we want to be in, for this gives us true freedom, lasting security, and transformative capability.

We start life in the random energy state and we can remain in that state throughout our lives. We can become set in our ways and too preoccupied to realize that we have the power to change. Some, through personal initiative, acquire the necessary skills to transform themselves into the directed energy state and, thus, improve their status in life. They are like liquids, resilient enough to move. They look beyond the immediate for ways to improve their lives. A few acquire the specific knowledge, specialized skills and enough maturity to graduate into the purposeful energy state and live leveraged and impactful lives.

HUMAN PYRAMID

Humans aren't as good as we should be in our capacity to empathize with feelings and thoughts of others, be they humans or other animals on Earth. So maybe part of our formal education should be training in empathy. Imagine how different the world would be if, in fact, that were 'reading, writing, arithmetic, empathy.'

— *Neil deGrasse Tyson*

It is convenient to put people in the three categories of random energy (gas), directed energy or force (liquid), and purposeful energy or power (solid). People, however, are not easily pigeonholed into discrete categories. Humans are complex. Each human is a mixture of solids, liquids and gases, a unique combination of energies, forces and powers. Each human has strengths and weaknesses.

There are many rungs on the helix of life. The one we occupy is somewhere between "earth", where we are and "heaven", our destination. Our status in life depends on our grade in the school of life. While some are in elementary school and others in secondary, a few are at the graduate level. Our challenges are our tests. They provide exactly what we need to learn and master before we can move on to the next grade.

And he dreamed, and behold, there was a ladder set up on the earth, and the top of it reached to heaven. And behold, the angels of God were ascending and descending on it!   Gen 28:12

According to John 14:2, Jesus said: *"In my Father's house are many rooms. If it were not so, would I have told you that I go to prepare a place for you?"* In the school of life, we determine which room, or what class, we place ourselves in and how long we stay there. Even though we start life on a particular rung, we do not have to remain there. We are expected to progress.

We have been admonished to know ourselves. This is a lifetime pursuit, for we are not as simple as we appear to be. In addition to our physical bodies, which can require years of study, we also have emotions, mind, history, past lives, hidden and obvious skills, abilities and a vast potential. On the surface, we seem to be a simple organism primed for survival. However, nothing is simple when it comes to humans. Even a thorough study of a mere cell can take a long time to complete.

We started life as a fertilized egg, but we rapidly progressed beyond that stage. We are ever changing. Currently, we are in a particular stage of our life cycle. With each developmental stage, we gain or lose functions, abilities, or skills. It is impossible to know us fully while we are still living. Perhaps a eulogy would best define us, for by then we would have completed this cycle. Just as we have lived through numerous days in this lifetime, we have lived multitudes of lives by way of reincarnation. Just as our focus is on today, so is our focus on this life-cycle. Our existence is cyclic. As souls, we had no beginning and will have no end. That is why it is difficult to know, or judge anyone. We cannot know a book by reading just one page. So, the best we can do to know ourselves, or anyone else, is to take a look at a snapshot, a frozen moment in space/time. That snapshot would be this lifetime.

Society is quick to judge individuals and fickle when it comes to attributing value to humans. Ideally, under the law, everyone is equal. The contributions of individuals to society, however, vary greatly. For a long time, athletes, entertainers, movie stars, politicians and military leaders were our heroes. All that changed with COVID-19 and the Coronavirus. Suddenly, the real heroes of society became obvious: the medical professionals who put their lives on the line to save patients; the EMT staff working prolonged hours; the truck drivers delivering food and essentials to stores; and the grocery store workers and cashiers risking exposure to the virus and yet, continuing to work so others may eat. A person's standing can change overnight. Yet what is far more important is the value we place on ourselves. How do we view ourselves? What is our standing in our own eyes?

We are a conglomeration of energies, forces and powers. We encompass multitudes of frequencies. We exist on several dimensions concurrently. However, we are mostly aware of only one level, where we are currently having an earthly human experience. Even though some stagnate on one level, most move up and down the human pyramid. No one is wholly on one level all the time. Most exhibit qualities from multiple levels. What characterizes a human being is the level of their consciousness and how well they use their freedom of choice. Whether our lives have been a success or a failure depends, not on what others say about us, but on how much we achieve based on our own criteria. The following are my criteria for the success of my life:

1. How many lives did I touch? What impact did I have on those lives?

2. How well did I guide the lives of my children? Did I do my best for them?

3. How good of a husband was I? How good of a friend or a neighbor was I?

4. How much love did I give and receive?

5. How much growth did I experience? Emotional growth where I accepted responsibility for my actions? Mental growth through continuous education? Spiritual growth through study and reflection?

6. How well did I use my time on earth to educate myself, cultivate my mind and build enduring relations? How much time did I waste?

7. Did I cause pain and suffering for anyone? How quickly did I recognize a fault in myself, apologize when wrong, and endeavor to do better?

8. How far did I move from harmful cultural influences, dogma and limiting beliefs? Did I let go of supersti-

tions, ignorance and fear? Did I act fearlessly when the situation warranted?

9. How long was I a blind follower/believer? How long was I an independent thinker?

10. How healthy, happy, and at peace was I?

11. How long did I have enough? How long was I financially secure?

12. How much of my divine potential did I actualize?

The world is different for different people. For some, it is a struggle to survive. For others, it is opulence and luxury. Even though it appears that people are having diverse experiences, life is an educational system in which everybody learns by experiencing.

To actualize our vast divine potential requires focus, intention and action that might necessitate several lifetimes to begin to scratch the surface. We are on a journey of self-discovery, a journey to divinity. Where we are on this journey depends on how much and for how long we have been working on raising our consciousness. Here is a brief look at the various rungs humans occupy. Like a pyramid, the base is wide, while the apex is narrow.

First Rung

People on the first rung live for themselves. They are self-centered and rarely think of others. Often, they bully the less fortunate. They are like a helium atom whose electrons revolve just around its protons. Life on the first floor is selfish, limited, and devoid of love and sympathy toward others. There is no creative thinking or originality at this level. Very few people are on this rung.

Second Rung

Expanding one's awareness to include another is existence on the second rung. Falling in love and increasing the sphere of one's awareness beyond the self, to include loved ones and the immediate family, is breaking the focus on self and enlarging it to include the welfare of others. There is very little creative thinking or originality at this level. Many are on this rung.

Third Rung

Expanding one's love, care, compassion, and sphere of interest to the extended family and the immediate community places us on the third rung of existence. Expanding our sphere of interest and being involved in our community adds another dimension to our lives. There is average creative thinking or originality at this level. Most people are on this rung.

Fourth Rung

Education, life lessons and travel add another dimension to our lives. Education broadens our perspectives, while life lessons help open our eyes and soften our hearts. Travel links our hearts and minds to others beyond our area. We get to know others as similar human beings, just like us, but in their own environments and under their unique circumstances.

Education, life lessons and travel are essential ingredients in the growth and maturation of an individual. People on the fourth rung take control of their lives and effect change. They are conceptual. They are free to set and change the course of their lives. They are usually experienced and mature. Creative thinking and originality are common place at this level. Many are on this rung.

Fifth Rung

People on the fifth rung do not have external authorities shaping their lives. Their internal authority instead, guides them: mind, heart, inspiration and *The Voice Within*. They live guided by ideals, such as justice, beauty, and excellence. People on the fifth rung are creative, able to generate new ideas, and can manifest that which they perceive and intend. They are at the helm of their ships and they are the creators of their future. Creative thinking and originality are abundant at this level. Fewer people are on this rung.

Sixth Rung

People on the sixth rung have mastery over their thoughts, emotions, and actions. They leverage their minds to easily achieve what they want. They employ reason, inspiration, contemplation, visualization, imagination and meditation to achieve whatever they set their minds and hearts to. They can direct their consciousness to heal and rejuvenate themselves and others. They are a force to be reckoned with. They have mastered creative thinking and are original. Few people are on this rung.

Seventh Rung

People on the seventh rung not only know who they are and who they have been, but they can decide to be whatever they choose. They have discovered their divinity and manifest it in their daily living. They have understanding, vision and compassion beyond measure. They see others for exactly who they are and where in their journey they happen to be. They never judge others. They live to awaken and empower. They are one with the environment, with others, and with their source, the God within and without. Very few people are on this rung.

Climbing up the human pyramid often entails moving two steps forward and one step backward. It is not a straightforward climb. There are many challenges and distractions along the way. Numerous routes lead to the top. Some are more direct than others and they take less time. However, they are much more demanding. Most choose to follow a longer and slower ascent. Each decides what is comfortable for them and sets their own course.

NATURAL "ENEMIES"
OF HUMANITY

For to win one hundred victories in one hundred battles is not the acme of skill. To subdue the enemy without fight is the acme of skill.

— *Sun Tzu*

An "enemy" is a perceived antagonist who can cause damage or harm. Often, when we think of an "enemy", we have an external entity in mind. However, damage and harm does not only come from an external enemy. There are far worse mental and emotional "enemies" that can cause long-lasting damage. These are internal "enemies." We have many "enemies", both personal and shared 'enemies."

Personal "Enemies"

Fighting an external enemy is a survival instinct. Who we consider to be an enemy is often obvious. Yet, frequently, our worst enemies are ourselves, what we harbor within. Having an external enemy keeps us on our toes, on edge, ready and prepared. Perhaps we can learn to be the same with our internal "enemies". Muslims have Jihad. Christians have the Crusade. These are often thought to be fights against perceived external enemies. There is, however, a deeper meaning to these terms. It is a Jihad and a Crusade against our own darker side, the unseen enemies residing within us. It is more difficult to face, challenge and obliterate an internal enemy. Facing an internal enemy requires resolve.

We each have our own challenges. These are our "crosses" to carry. For some, it is establishing clearly defined boundaries. For others, it is anger management. Some need to learn to love themselves, be able to receive graciously, or learn not to be a victim. Others need to gain courage and speak their truth. A few need to stop blaming others, accept personal responsibility, and work on their self-esteem.

Internal "enemies" are not only what we perceive as negatives, such as hatred, jealousy, envy, greed, destructive habits, negative attitudes and debilitating beliefs. These need to be brought to the light, faced, and vanquished. Internal "enemies" could also include what is positive. Some people are so good that their goodness becomes their "enemy." There are some who are all heart. They are too giving and enable others instead of assisting and empowering them. This makes it easy for others to take advantage of them. Beauty and perfection of character come from a flawless symphony of balanced traits and characteristics that work together seamlessly.

Shared "Enemies"

There are various types of external shared enemies: enemies that threaten, attack, or harm us. There are also enemies of war, political enemies and enemies of the state. These are people who are hostile, oppose, and who can cause damage. Even though our shared external adversaries are diverse, humanity, in general, has a few common internal "enemies". Here are five that we need to face, combat and vanquish.

1. Boredom
2. Disease, Pain and Suffering
3. Fear
4. Ignorance
5. Justification

1. Boredom

The worst boredom I experienced was when I was in the Army at Ft. Meade, MD. The weekends and holidays were very tough for me. Almost everyone would leave to go visit family and friends. I was alone and without a car. Driven by boredom, I would take a bus to Baltimore and aimlessly walk the streets for hours and then take the bus back to the base.

Boredom is a natural indicator that a change is needed, a call for the introduction of something interesting, stimulating or challenging. It is as if the life we are living is bland and requires something to spice it up. If understood as such, boredom can lead to creativity, constructive change and achievement. Repetitive actions can and do lead to boredom; so does the absence of value and meaning in what we do. These are human characteristics that distinguish us from machines that can repeat mindless acts indefinitely. For us, lack of meaning and the accumulation of repetitive actions "weigh" heavily on us and dull the senses. They lead to boredom. Laziness, aversion to contribute, and lack of passion can also lead to boredom. Boredom is instilled within us by nature to help propel us to action. The antidote to boredom is involvement, adding interest to our activities, and making believe that what we are engaged in is important. We can pretend that what we are doing is a game and that we are having fun. Pretending can fool the mind into believing.

Our world is too beautiful and full of interesting things for anyone to ever get bored. There are books to read, games to play, skills to acquire or develop, people and places to visit. Often, a simple walk in nature will do. Since creativity is an integral aspect of human nature, boredom is the signal that it is time to be creative.

2. Disease, Pain And Suffering

Generally speaking, I have been very healthy. Once, I got up at night to go to the bathroom. I do not remember exactly what I did to cause the onslaught of severe back pain. I was bending for some reason and suddenly, as if a switch was flicked off, I collapsed to the floor and could not move. This was the most incapacitating experience I have ever had. It took me, what seemed like over an hour to crawl to the bathroom.

Avoiding disease, pain and suffering are not easy because we are feeling and emotional beings. Unless we get sick, feel pain, and experience suffering we do not do what it takes to avoid them. Staying healthy to avoid misery is a personal responsibility. It requires intelligence, awareness, inspiration, self-control and constructive habits.

While debilitating disease, prolonged pain and suffering weaken, age and lead to the body's demise, minor experiences of these are beneficial. They help to awaken us, teach us, and strengthen our immune system. While on my world cruise, I was exposed to the germs of people from many countries that I had never encountered before. I succumbed to some of them. However, with some rest, in a few days my body recovered and I was back to normal. This experience has transformed me into an international person with immunity against many types of germs. Getting sick and experiencing pain once in a while is normal, natural, and beneficial. It is a feedback mechanism to let us know how we are doing.

A strong, healthy body's reaction to the onset of disease is very different from a body that is weakened or unhealthy. We must always assume the responsibility for keeping our bodies healthy. We must do what is within our power to aid our bodies. This includes having proper nutrition and hygiene, getting enough exercise and rest, and maintaining a positive mental attitude. We must also keep our emotions, mind and spirit healthy, unencumbered and joyful.

There are times when suffering is beyond our control. What if we have family members who through their behavior cause us unimaginable and prolonged suffering? What if we are born destitute and suffer as a result? What if we inherit genetic propensities for diseases that manifest and cause us suffering?

I have learned that when we suffer, we are not suffering for ourselves alone. If we become better human beings as a result of suffering, if we grow and mature because of our suffering, if we become more compassionate and understanding of others because we suffered, then, the benefits of our suffering are not limited to ourselves alone. If we improve, the lives we touch are better as a result. If their lives become better, the future generations benefit as well.

Imagine a mother suffering and sacrificing to help educate her daughter. The benefit of her sacrifice is not limited to her and her daughter. Once the daughter has a better life, future generations of that daughter will fare better as well. The results of our actions cascade to future generations.

3. Fear

The most intense fear I experienced was when our young daughter was very sick and struggling to breathe. I remember sitting by her open door at night, listening intently to hear her breathing, afraid it might stop.

Fear can be conscious or it can be hidden and subconscious. While small doses of fear are cautionary, debilitating fears and phobias are not. Many have unrealistic fears, such as the fear of death, punishment, God, self-expression, commitment and the unknown. These fears can be overcome but require understanding and a desire to take action to dispel them.

As children, it is natural to experience fear. Once we become adults, it behooves us to critically examine our self-induced fears. Fear-based beliefs, such as fear of God, punishment or even death can and should be replaced with more illuminated ones. All beliefs, without exception, must be examined and evaluated through critical thinking.

The root cause of many fears is a sense of helplessness, often in the face of an unknown. We are afraid of death because we do not know what will happen. We fear public speaking because we lack self-confidence and are unsure of how we will be received. We fear God because we believe in a judgmental deity. We fear natural phenomenon, such as storms and volcanoes, because we feel helpless. We fear creatures such as snakes and spiders because of what they can do to us. Our imagination plays a major role in our fears. We seem unable to control our thoughts. Instead of focusing on what we fear or unlikely events, we can focus on the positive aspects of ourselves and visualize the outcomes we want.

Fear is an emotion. It has a powerful impact on the body. It can paralyze us into inaction and compromise the immune system. We cannot eliminate fear through reasoning or logical analysis. Fear is an energy that must be transformed or transmuted. Here is a 4-step process to transform and overcome fear:

First, we must realize that fear is a conglomerate of pictures, emotions, feelings, thoughts and projections stored in the mind and the body. Fear is a package of energies. Energy can never be destroyed. It can, however, be transformed. It is true that what we focus on, we empower. Therefore, we should dwell on what we want and not what we fear.

Second, we can transform the energy of fear. Employing visualization, imagination and self-talk, we can change the nature of the energy of fear from negative to positive. We can replace fear-inducing images with empowering outcomes. For comprehensive instructions on how to do this, please refer to Stage 6 in my book: *A Passion for Living, A Path to Meaning and Joy.*

Third, we must understand that the object of living is not safety and isolation. It is to have a variety of experiences, some of which are unpleasant. We are not created by a God and placed on Earth to be tormented by fear. Know that we are part of the divine creator, here by choice, to experience and reflect our divinity. We are truly free to choose and create the life we desire, devoid of fear. By employing visualization and imagination, we can transform and transmute that which we do not want and replace it with what we desire to experience.

Fear of death is instinctive, but unnatural. The truth is that we are eternal. We have absolutely nothing to fear even if we lose our lives, for we have lived and died many times before. We have divinity residing within us. When the divine is in us, what is there to fear? We are souls in a body. Our bodies are temporary. We are forever.

Fourth, fear enslaves, binds, and stifles the joy of living. There is no true freedom where fear exists.

We can never fully experience life if we are gripped and paralyzed by fear. We must take deliberate action to confront our fears. We can use crutches initially, if we must. Then we must throw away those crutches. Repeating small positive steps leads to the formation of habits, which over time, become second nature. Successful actions build self-confidence. Confidence transforms us and is often all we lack.

4. Ignorance

The problem with ignorance is that we do not know that we are ignorant when we are. It is only later that we realize our ignorance. While living in Syria, my world was very limited. I was totally ignorant about the rest of the world. Living in Lebanon decreased my ignorance. Ignorance, however, never completely disappears.

Ignorance is like an uncultivated field. Mostly useless weeds grow in neglected fields. Ignorance is a difficult enemy to combat, for we do not know that we are ignorant until we become enlightened. As long as we have unexamined beliefs instead of knowledge, we remain ignorant. We adopt and follow many systems. Instead of using these systems as temporary space holders, we get bound and trapped by them. Religion dictates what we should believe, while science sets the boundaries of what we can accept as true. To be free of ignorance, we must be open-minded. We must accept that we do not know everything. We must act like a bee drifting from plant to plant, gathering nectar wherever we find it. Systems should be a means for acquiring knowledge and not a method of control and setting limitations. By continuously educating ourselves, by living and experiencing, the scales of ignorance will fall from our eyes, minds, and hearts. We will see clearly without a veil and we will become enlightened.

5. Justification

The above four enemies of humanity are natural, evident and obvious. Boredom; disease, pain and suffering; fear and ignorance all have remedies. The fifth enemy of mankind is pervasive and harder to combat. Justification is showing something to be right or reasonable. We all engage in justifying our actions because we do not want to be wrong, appear incompetent, or even be seen as evil. Murders, injustices, and prejudices are perpetrated and justified. We are very talented at explaining away anything. Even Hitler justified his actions; so do mass murderers, robbers and habitual liars. The only hope we have of improving is if we stop justifying our reprehensible actions. We must learn to admit our shortcomings, confess our mistakes and resolve to do and be better. Justification is a veil we place in front of us to cover up the obvious. With justification, our blinders are in place. Even though we have eyes, we do not see what is so obvious and even though we have ears, we cannot hear the truth of a situation. Justification is what makes us the people Christ referred to as having eyes that do not see and ears that do not hear. By justifying that "Christ came to die for our sins" we killed not only Him, but countless others as well.

According to the Bible, the habit of justifying, finding excuses and blaming others started in a garden.

In this garden, the final blame was placed upon the serpent, also known as the devil or Satan. It was Eve who decided to eat the fruit. It was Adam who chose to eat, after his partner offered him some of the fruit. The serpent did not force either to do anything against their will. In the final analysis, the buck stops with us. We must stop justifying, or blaming others for the choices we made. We must accept responsibility for our actions.

◆ ◆ ◆

Newton's first law of motion is often stated as "an object at rest stays at rest and an object in motion stays in motion with the same speed and in the same direction unless acted upon by an unbalanced force." (The Physics Classroom). This may be seen as a statement about inertia, but it is also true about us. It is natural for many to continue to live careless and haphazard lives, not caring for their bodies, minds and spirits unless and until a force acts upon them to make them think and change course. For most, this is disease, pain and suffering. Often, we do not realize the value of something until we lose it. Unless there is a force to stop us, we will continue our bad habits: eating excessively, abusing our bodies, and avoiding exercise. The forces that propel us out of our inertia are our natural "enemies." These "enemies" are our friends in disguise. That is why Christ taught us to love our enemies. We need to transform these natural enemies into best friends. We can use boredom to spring into action, creativity and productivity. We can remember our pain and suffering from disease and resolve to stay healthy and maintain our vitality. We can transmute our fears into determination and courage. We can change our ignorance into knowledge and a continued pursuit of enlightenment. We can stop justifying our actions by deciding to see ourselves as we truly are, imperfect, but with so much good within us. We can easily eliminate our deficiencies if only we stop justifying and start living in truth. By accepting responsibility for our lives, we demonstrate our adulthood and maturity.

PART TWO

◆ ◆ ◆

STRUGGLE

MEMORY AS A PHOTOGRAPH

You don't take a photograph, you make it.

— Ansel Adams

As I write this chapter, I am sitting in our ship, "Columbus", viewing the ocean waters of New Zealand. I am enjoying the view from the dome on the 14th floor. The ship is sailing towards Australia. It is exactly 10:39 a.m.

Will this moment last? Absolutely not. It is already 10:40 a.m. Everything is in motion. We cannot arrest this movement. We cannot step into the same river twice. This is because the changing coordinates of space/time make it impossible to do so. Even if we stand still, remaining in the same space, time is ticking and we are constantly in a new timeframe.

We can, however, capture what we deem as significant by taking a mental or actual picture and storing it as memory. Each picture is an instance in space/time that acts as a trigger for events, with associated memories and emotions.

One of the most cherished photographs I have is an autographed picture of President Barack Obama. It simply states: "To Shahan, Best Wishes. Barack Obama." What happens when I look at this picture? I feel moved and I feel pride. A picture conjures up memories and emotions.

A picture freezes a specific moment in space and time. It captures the scene we focus on and its environment. Pictures are two-dimensional. They are a cross section of a multi-dimensional event. Each picture elicits a selective bundle of memories. Memories are subject to various recollections and interpretations.

I have pictures of different times and places, some are meaningful, while others are not. I have pictures of my children at various stages of their lives and pictures of places I have visited or lived in. I have pictures of nature, family, friends, and events. **Pictures are triggers for memories and emotions**.

I also have memories of various times and places, some are meaningful, while others are not. I have memories of my children at different stages of their lives and memories of places I have visited or lived in. I have recollections of nature, family, friends, and events. **Memories are like pictures. They are triggers for events and emotions**.

Our past is a storehouse of pictures and memories. Some believe that we can never change our past because what transpired is forever gone. Yet, we store what happened in the past, or what happens now, as pictures or memories. These trigger specific emotions because of how we interpret what took place. What if we control the interpretation and decide the meaning and value of a memory whenever we remember it, so that it serves our need to grow, unfold, and mature? We have "good and happy" memories and we have "sad and not so good" memories. Happy or sad memories are so because we think of them as such. Our power resides in what we choose to make of what happened, based on our interpretation and the value we assign to an event.

We can look at painful memories and sublimate them – extracting value from them or conferring "better" interpretations upon them. We can transform them to serve our growth. This can free us from their bondage and allow us to more fully enjoy life. We can choose not to be victims of circumstance because we have the power to reinterpret stored memories. No one can tell us what our memories mean. We are free to interpret these memories in a way that serves us. It is our right and it is our responsibility to take care of ourselves by actively managing our memories.

It is best to not dwell on events where we were victims. Instead we can change our memories and remember ourselves as heroes. We can look at all of our experiences and memories as photographs. It is imperative that we see ourselves as the photographers. We hold the camera. We choose the scenes we capture. We determine the value and the meaning of the photograph through our interpretations.

It is the same with our experiences. We are the experiencers. Our interpretations determine the meaning of an experience. We must not give up this ability by allowing "others" to determine the value and meaning of an event for us. It is our responsibility and obligation to determine the outcome of what happens to us. By molding what happens to us into whatever we need to learn, to grow, and to mature, we recreate ourselves. We can each become an alchemist for our lives by reinterpreting our past, deciding our current experiences and molding our future through the actions we take today. If a picture is worth a thousand words and an experience worth ten thousand, then mining our minds (pictures, memories and experiences) for value is worth a million.

Trauma

Many of us have experienced traumas in our lives. These are stored in our consciousness as memories and as pictures, with associated emotions. We have assigned meaning and given specific values to these experiences, oftentimes mostly negative. We have the power to reassign new meanings and values to these experiences. We can extract good from any event, even very painful ones. We can transform and transmute our traumas to get the most value out of them, value that serves not only our interests but that of humanity as well. Once we repeatedly change our interpretations, over time, the associated emotions change as well. We are powerful if we choose to take action. We can act now to reshape our past for a better future.

GOOD, BAD AND EVIL

Nature has no principles. She makes no distinction between good and evil.

— *Anatole France*

While living in Beirut, Lebanon, I knew two American women who were polar opposites. Aunt Faith, a Presbyterian missionary, was involved with my family when my mother worked for her as a maid in Aleppo, Syria. Aunt Faith's life was guided by her religion and the Bible. For her, there was only one right understanding of the Bible, hers. She was very conservative. One time, I wanted to take my sister to the movies. She wanted me to see the movie alone first, to make sure there was no kissing in the movie. Even though she had lived in the Middle East for many years, she never understood the culture. Another time, my brother John invited his boss over for dinner at my Aunt's place. When we sat down to eat, my Aunt served the boss a tiny amount of food and told him that he could have more once he finished his portion. We were appalled. He was insulted. He never visited us again. Our relationship with her was that of parent-to-child. We were the children. She was the parent.

Jean, a family friend, was very different. Even though we knew her for a shorter time, her impact on me was enormous. I had an adult-to-adult relationship with her. While my Aunt and I argued over religion, Jean never discussed religion with me. While my Aunt bragged to everyone about helping us, Jean never let anyone know what she was doing. Jean loaned me money to go to college. No one ever knew about that. She often went to visit my brothers and sister in the orphanage. She would take them out to movies and public swimming pools, and have picnics with us without ever letting anyone know what she did. Jean was instrumental in our coming to the U.S. It was easy for me to consider Jean as a mother.

It would be natural for me to think of Jean and my Aunt as examples of good and bad, but that would be a mistake. Aunt Faith, who grew up during the Depression, was greatly influenced by her parents. They were very religious. She was an only child who did not get married until very late in life. She always did the best she knew how. Jean was different. She was not religious, was married with four children, and was free-spirited. She was the example of a mature adult. I am glad I knew them both. Now that I am more mature, I realize that good, bad and evil are relative terms.

In the Lord's Prayer, we ask God to deliver us from evil. But what exactly is evil? Evil is defined as and is synonymous with: wicked, bad, wrong, profoundly immoral, sinful and many other terms. In the West, we seem to struggle with the concept of good and evil. God is good while the devil is evil. For us, anyone or anything can be good, bad or evil. We seem to believe in a duality, a struggle between the two forces of good and evil. We even believe that there will be a judgment day, a reckoning between God and the devil, and that God will be victorious. We are raised to believe in separation. We have light and dark, good and evil, male and female, human and God, life and death. These dualities are not separate. They are two aspects of the same reality, perhaps at opposite poles, but often comingled like a coin that has two sides yet is one entity. We look at a coin from one side and we see a "head." We look at it from the other side and we see a "tail." It is the same with any opposites including life and death. There is only one doorway; we enter it one way and we are born. We go through it the other way and we die. It is the same doorway.

The word God comes from the Germanic word, which stands for good. This meaning creates problems and leads to confusion. The moment we say "good," we think of evil, because they are two sides of the same coin. Good and evil go hand-in-hand. Good seems to be what we want, while evil is what we want to be delivered from. To deliver means to rescue and to set free. In some other parts of the world, the concept of 'God as good' does not exist. God embodies unity. God is all there is or ever will be.

We need to have a better understanding of what we mean by good, bad and evil. The Bible contains references about this concept in the Garden of Eden. We are admonished not to eat of the fruit of the Tree of Knowing Good and Evil. The Syriac word for good is "Tobo" while the word for evil is "Beesho." (Syriac is a form of Aramaic.) "Tobo" can mean good, but it also has several other meanings, such as valuable, precious, worth something, cultivated, mature, ripe, excellent, honorable, kind, gracious, benevolent, beneficent or favorable. "Beesho", on the other hand, can mean not only evil but also bad, ugly, error, cruel, mistake, malignant, rotten, unripe, immature, unfortunate, unlucky, wicked, wrong, diseased, incorrect, culprit, deceiver, troublemaker, or the evil one.

There is a reference in Jeremiah, Chapter 24 beginning with verse 1, that talks about "Tobo" (what we call good) and "Beesho" (what we term evil) in two totally different contexts. The second context is closer to the deeper meaning of good and evil that I believe was the original intent. Here is that passage from two different translations. I will only include the pertinent part, skipping the filler information.

First translation:

The LORD showed me two baskets of figs placed before the temple of the LORD. ---One basket had very good figs, like first-ripe figs, but the other basket had very bad figs, so bad that they could not be eaten.

And the LORD said to me, "What do you see, Jeremiah?" I said, "Figs, the good figs very good, and the bad figs very bad, so bad that they cannot be eaten."   Jeremiah 24:1-3

Here is the second translation. It makes the meaning of the words good and bad very clear:

And Yahweh said to me: "What do you see, Jeremiah?" and I replied: "Figs, ripe figs, very ripe

*figs; and unripe figs, very unripe figs, no one can
eat them because they are so sour."*

The words used to describe the figs in one version
of the Bible translated them as good and bad, while the
second version correctly translated them as ripe and
unripe. While figs are ripe or unripe, people are neither
good nor bad; rather, they are mature or immature. In
other words, most of the "good" people we face are mature people, while some of the most difficult people we
encounter are immature people.

Here is another example of the use of the terms
good and evil:

When Christ says: "I am the Good Shepherd",
what does it mean to be a good shepherd? Does it mean
that Christ is not a bad or an evil shepherd?

According to Zecharia Sitchin, author of the
Earth Chronicles books, Sumerian rulers cherished the
title En.Si that means "Righteous Ruler." (The 12th
Planet page 23). The first king to bear this title was Sar-
gon the first, a common gardener and shepherd selected
by the goddess Inanna to be king of Sumer and Akkad.
This ruler was righteous, just, and compassionate. He
used the law to direct human conduct, rather than punish human faults. In fact, this king bore the name-epi-
thet **Sharru-Kin**, meaning righteous king. The king was
known as the "**Righteous Shepherd.**"

So, when Christ says: "I am the Good Shepherd",
He is stating that He is righteous and good. More importantly, He is a mature shepherd of the people. Christ
is the light within. This light within is the same mature *Voice Within*. As for people, there are only mature

and immature people. Obviously, there are people who do bad and evil deeds. Are these people evil? Not from their point of view. For they justify their actions, like we all do. Good and evil are on the opposite rungs of the ladder of consciousness. While humans at high levels of consciousness exhibit goodness and maturity, humans at low levels of consciousness exhibit evil and immaturity.

Good and bad are generic terms. We should stop using them. Instead, we should use more descriptive terms. Christ, referring to trees, said that by their fruit you shall know them. (Matt 7:20). The "fruit" of immaturity is selfishness, fear, and ignorance. These are the guiding principles of an immature person. The "fruit" of maturity, on the other hand, is wisdom, knowledge, altruism, and courage. These are the guiding principles of a mature person.

Immature means not being ripe or ready. It is not a permanent state. Given enough time and spiritual light, any person will slowly ripen, mature and be ready. Being immature is like having obstructed vision. Immature people have tunnel vision, which limits and distorts their view. This might shed some light on the parable of the ten virgins who were waiting for the groom with lamps. The five virgins who were prepared and ready were labeled "wise virgins"; in other words, mature. While the other five, who were not, were labeled "foolish", or immature. (Matthew 25:1-13).

Those of us with children know how tough it can be to deal with teens and young adults. These are difficult years for relationships. This is because our children, and many times we ourselves are not mature enough to have meaningful relationships. We have not had sufficient and pertinent experiences to be mature.

We are also often immature when it comes to dealing with people. We are like Jeremiah's figs in the second basket: green, unripe, and immature. To become like the good figs – ripe, sweet, and delicious – requires persevering through a great deal of difficulties and challenges. For it is only through slogging the furnace of tough experiences and the fire of difficulties, pain, and suffering that we will be exposed to the sun's warming rays, and slowly and surely ripen and mature. Our challenges are the cross upon which our personality unfolds, blossoms, and matures.

In the Lord's Prayer, when we ask God to deliver us from evil, the best way to set ourselves free of evil is not to avoid it, but rather to face evil and transform it into good. We should ask for the insight, the wisdom, and the understanding to deal with evil (immaturity) and convert it into an opportunity to do good and hasten maturity.

Is nature good, bad or even evil? Can something as simple as the weather be good or bad? When the weather behaves according to our wishes, we term the situation good. When things do not meet our expectations or fulfill our desires, we term the situation bad. This happens when it rains too much or not enough or when it is too cold or too hot. Obviously, it is not the weather that is good or bad, it is our perception of it.

I once read about an old Sufi who had a son and a horse. One day, the horse took off and disappeared. People came to the Sufi and said, "It's too bad that your horse is gone." The Sufi answered, "Perhaps."

In a few days, the horse returned with a beautiful mare and the people came to the Sufi and told him, "It is so good that your horse returned with a mare." The Sufi answered, "Perhaps."

The next day his son broke his leg while attempting to tame the mare. People came to the Sufi and said to him, "It is too bad that your son broke his leg." The Sufi answered, "Perhaps."

In a few days, soldiers appeared in the village gathering conscripts for the army. They took all the young men, but left the Sufi's son because of his broken leg. The people once more came to the Sufi and said to him, "How wonderful that your son was not taken with the soldiers." The Sufi answered, "Perhaps."

We should discontinue using the term "evil" to describe people. It is more appropriate to use the term "immature" instead. The difference between **immaturity and evil** is more than semantics. Once we term someone or something as evil, that becomes its identity. It has been labeled as such and will always be so. Calling someone or something immature, instead, allows for the hope that, over time, maturity can occur. Immaturity is imbued with hope while evil implies hopelessness.

Maturity, immaturity, good, bad and evil are all a matter of perspective. Over time – sometimes over a long period of time – the good in all becomes evident. Even floods, fires, and volcanoes eventually produce a great deal of good. They renew, invigorate, and introduce new life to our planet.

So it is with our lives. Eventually, and after a long time, it becomes evident that all is good and everything is unfolding as it should. Everything is a component of a great plan, an engineering marvel that is the handiwork of a great intelligent consciousness that is all pervasive.

TRANSFORMERS OF THE WORLD

To be a monk is to have time to practice for your transformation and healing. And after that to help with the transformation and healing of other people.

— *Thick Nhat Hanh*

When I joined the US Army at Ft. Meade, MD, I was shy, self-conscious and very respectful of authority, especially officers. My basic training at Ft. Dix, NJ had inculcated that in me. At Ft. Meade, I befriended Roger, the photographer, who was exactly what I needed for a transformation in attitude. Roger was the consummate, self-assured extrovert. For him, officers were just like him deserving no more or less respect than anyone else. Spending three years with Roger transformed me into a self-assured, confident person.

Transformation is different from change in that it is permanent. There is no going back. While change is often superficial, transformation is profound. While change is ongoing, transformation is sporadic or sudden. It can occur as a result of events, people or bold action. Accumulated changes often lead to transformation. An example of transformation in nature is the metamorphosis of a caterpillar into a butterfly. Even more of a miracle is the transformation of a crude, rude, immature human into a loving, mature, angelic being.

I have experienced both sudden and slow transformations. An example of a sudden transformative event, with permanent impact, was the sudden and unexpected death of my mother at the age of 36. I was 13 years old. With no mother to keep us together, our sense of family and security was shattered and we were scattered to different locations.

Each of us has undergone several transformations. We appear to be self-made, autonomous individuals, but we are not. Biologically, we are the combination of native cells and "foreign" bacteria. Genetically, we are native genome and "foreign" viral DNA. Emotionally, mentally, culturally and spiritually, we are our own creations along with the contributions of others. We are a conglomerate of native and "foreign" elements. We are one, yet a collectivity. We are what we created ourselves to be, and what others have contributed to our being. We are dynamic beings, transformed by others and, in turn, transforming many others. My life is the transformative impact many had on me. Jean made it possible for me to go to college. Dr. Norman Frigerio opened my mind to skepticism and bold questioning in college. The U.S. Army provided me with opportunities I would not have had otherwise. Yet, the greatest transformative impact on my life was the slow, cumulative positive impact of continuous education.

There are two types of transformations: individual transformation, which is personal, and global transformation, which impacts everyone. In ancient times, life was difficult. People struggled to survive. They did not have the tools and implements to make life easy and comfortable. Humanity was not as connected and required great events or disruptive inventions to transform humanity and the world. Then the breakthroughs began to happen and slowly but surely, our world and humanity was transformed. Here are some of the events and individuals who contributed to our transformation:

Language

The transition from grunts to vocalization was a transformative event for humanity. The invention of language, reading, writing and printing changed our world. The invention of the printing press made books available to everyone. Common people could now read and acquire knowledge directly through the printed material. Once we learned to communicate and document our achievements, we created history. We began to build on our past, learn from our mistakes, and make progress. Using symbols, analogies, similes, and metaphors was important in developing our mind and expanding our consciousness. Conceptual thinking made rapid advancements possible.

Agriculture

With the discovery of agriculture and animal husbandry, people could settle and have enough food and free time for leisure and introspection, a truly transformative event. Free time impels curiosity and leads to creative discoveries.

Religion

The various major religions, such as Hinduism, Zoroastrianism, Buddhism, Judaism, Christianity and Islam had a major impact on humanity and transformed our world, as did various beliefs, ideas, and philosophies. Religion taught morality and a belief in reward and punishment and helped elevate the moral and behavioral status of humanity. Religion attributed causes of natural and personal events to gods and goddesses or to a single God. While repressive religion ushered in the Dark Ages, its backlash gave rise to the Renaissance and the Age of Enlightenment.

Science and Technology

Science, engineering, technology, specialization and industrialization transformed, not only our lives, but the planet as well. The technology we create and use makes our lives easier and more comfortable. Now we have many specialized tools that can tackle almost any task. We can travel quickly, communicate effortlessly and live in luxury. The scientific method ensures that common, defensible facts prevail. Medicine keeps us healthy and extends our lives. Specialization increases productivity, efficiency and leads to a higher standard of living. Industrialization gives us better and cheaper products, increases our wealth and allows us to enjoy healthier life styles.

The Arts

Music, art, and literature enrich our lives beyond measure. They transform our drab "black and white" world into one of vibrant colors. The arts preserve our history, expand our emotions, and enable our spirits to soar. Music makes our spirit dance. Songs buoy and connect us to humanity. Paintings evoke deep emotions within us and cathedrals fill us with awe. Literature helps us understand past events, connects us to great minds, and frees our imagination to soar.

Natural Disasters, Pandemics, War

Cataclysmic events transform human lives and the planet. We have had several pandemics with disastrous consequences, the latest of which is COVID-19. Pandemics, earthquakes, floods and hurricanes reshape humanity and our planet. We have lived through devastating wars. Earth has been hit by many meteorites, some which caused extinctions.

Unique Individuals

Inventions such as the printing press, electricity, the telephone, transportation modes, the assembly line, computers and electronics are the contributions of unique, dedicated and highly talented individuals. The value of these contributions is felt in our everyday lives. They transformed us from primitives into cultured people. Unique individuals are the movers and shakers of society. They are the pillars that support the community and the arrows that lead the way and advance humanity. A few such unique individuals are Thomas Edison, Nikola Tesla, Bill Gates, Steve Jobs, and Elon Musk. Others, such as Gandhi and Martin Luther King Jr., had a transformative impact on how we relate to one another.

Impactful Experiences

We are individually transformed when we have impactful experiences such as the birth of a child, death of a loved one, unexpected events such as winning the lottery, and the onset of an incurable disease. These events unalterably transform our lives. Most often, with transformation comes maturity, newness and an opportunity for a fresh start.

Climate Change

Climate change impacts agriculture when the water supply declines causing reduced agricultural yields. Flooding and coastal erosion cause people to migrate. Increased heat and drought affect human health. Insect plagues devastate plants. Climate change is a slow, but certain transformative agent.

You and Me

These are some of the factors that transformed humanity and our world in the past. It is different now. Our world is much more connected and a small change in one area has a ripple effect everywhere. Now **we are the Transformers of the World**. It is a fact that, via entanglement and quantum existence, we are impacting and influencing each other, whether or not we are aware of it. The effects of our thoughts, feelings and actions are global. We exist in one world united by a quantum field that envelops us all. An act of generosity, kindness and philanthropy in one area impacts the world in its entirety. We are the transformers of the world. Let us roll up our sleeves and get involved to make a difference. Let us ever be aware of the power we possess, the responsibility we have, and the impact we can have on our world. Even a smile, a kind gesture, or a selfless act can transform the world.

PERFECTION

The essence of being human is that one does not seek perfection.

—*George Orwell*

I am glad I am not perfect. My life in the monastery in Lebanon was idyllic. All I had to do was study, pray and contemplate. I was liked by all, especially the head of the monastery, Father Saka. On Sundays, we went to the local church and participated in the mass that was in Syriac, a form of Aramaic. The mass included lots of chanting. Everyone had a good, or at least an acceptable voice, except for me. My voice was dreadful and no one wanted to hear me chant. Because of my poor voice, eventually I left the monastery to continue my education elsewhere.

To be perfect is to be free from flaws, defects and blemishes. If we accept that to be human is to be imperfect, and that the reason we are here on earth is to work on our flaws and imperfections, then perhaps we will realize that our experiences are the ideal opportunities to face and eliminate our deficiencies. Living and experiencing is the preferred method to progress toward perfection. As with my poor voice, often our deficiencies are the guideposts directing us away from our current situation toward new ventures that employ our strengths and passions instead.

The statement: "No one is perfect but God" is true. No one is perfect is a statement we should take to heart. If no one is perfect, then **we** are not perfect. We are born and grow up with a mixed bag of good and not-so-good attributes. We have our challenges. Each of us has his or her own cross to carry. Because we have our shortfalls, we cannot be judgmental of others. In fact, not being perfect teaches us humility and compassion.

Christ admonishes us to be perfect, as our heavenly Father is perfect (Matt 5:48). This implies that we are not perfect, but should try to be. Trying to be perfect is the purpose of living. The fact that we are not perfect affords us a golden opportunity. We can improve. There is work that needs to be done. Many of our challenges are opportunities in disguise, waiting for us to recognize them and then take action and, as a result, improve.

Our journey is that of gradual improvement. We are like a block of stone waiting to be stripped of impurities to reveal the glorious individual buried within. Living and experiencing is chiseling away at our rough exterior to liberate a polished, sparkling interior. We are like clay in the hands of a skilled potter. The potter, in our case, is life. Our experiences, especially the challenging ones, are the cross upon which our weaknesses are exposed, our personality unfolds, and our character blossoms. It is easy to believe that we are perfect when we are young and full of vigor. However, it is during our low points that we are reminded that we are not perfect or all powerful. This happens when we are sick, weak, and debilitated, unable to perform the simplest of tasks.

We are human, from God's essence, but not gods yet. We are not perfect. Therefore, let us practice forgiveness, tolerance, patience, understanding and compassion toward both ourselves and others. Perfection is an ideal. Ideals are goals to strive for, and to realize that they can never be fully attained. As long as we are human, we will remain imperfect. Accept it and be at peace with it without giving up the desire to improve. Once in a while, we get a fleeting glimpse of perfection, perhaps as an incentive that it exists and that we should continue to strive to attain it. I have been stunned by perfect beauty at least twice. It left an indelible mark on my consciousness. But alas, physical beauty does not last.

Just as the body slowly grows all its parts at the same time, so must our progress toward perfection grow slowly. The body does not grow hands, then feet, then heart and slowly the other organs. All growth takes place simultaneously. Perfection is not only freedom from physical flaws and defects. It is the blossoming and maturing of our character, personality, qualities and abilities, all making progress concurrently. There is nothing more beautiful than a physically stunning, emotionally mature, mentally well-developed, and spiritually illumined human being.

WHY ATTRACTION? WHY LOVE?

Wisdom begins in wonder.

—Socrates

A seed in the ground attracts to itself what it needs to grow.

A human involved with life attracts what that individual needs to grow.

A flower provides nectar to bees so pollination may ensue.

Life provides pleasure to humans so attraction and love is pursued.

Life's ultimate purpose in attraction, love, sex and pleasure is the perpetuation of the species. The unintended consequences for an individual are growth and maturation.

Attraction and love are not random for an individual. They are specific. We do not get attracted and fall in love with just anybody. It is usually someone special.

So, who attracts us? Why? Why do we fall in love? Have you ever wondered why you were attracted to the specific person you fell in love with and, perhaps, married? I have, often.

My attraction to and love of my wife was, and is, so I may encounter my shortcomings, face them, learn important lessons from them, resolve issues and grow into a mature adult. In other words, I was and am attracted to my wife specifically, to work on my deficiencies, perfect my character, and gain mastery over certain situations. I believe that we attract, not only the situations, but also the people we need to learn through, build a life with, and grow with. Obviously, this is in addition to the love, affection and pleasure we share and enjoy. These are the nectar that brings us together in the first place.

Life is the flower for which love is the honey.

— Victor Hugo

Attraction and love are nature's way of bringing people together so that life continues and improvements can take place. Who we love and are attracted to strikes a sympathetic chord in our being, triggers a change, and raises our vibratory frequency so high that, at times, we feel light enough to float.

With attraction and love comes attachment. With attachment comes the likelihood of disappointment and hurt. Far too often, the ones closest to us are the ones who can cause us the most pain. Perhaps that is why the Buddha admonished us against attachments. Yet, without attachment, we cannot experience intimacy. We cannot feel intense pleasure. If we practice detachment to avoid pain, we also shield ourselves from love. We stop learning and growing.

Learning and growing makes me happy because it leads to maturity. We do not mature easily or quickly. Chiseling away at our imperfections to reveal the beauty within is painful, exhausting, and at times, devastating. We suffer because we hang on to what we believe to be part of our identity, when it is just excessive ego. At times, we are tempted to give up, quit and abandon our engagement all together. This could be a mistake. To make sure that we stay on track and not deviate, we have a guide, a beacon urging us to see the deeper implications of our experiences. This guide is *The Voice Within*. If we heed its promptings, it will direct us to our most appropriate outcomes. There are no guarantees that we will succeed, however. We, and those involved, can behave against our best interests. *The Voice Within* can lead us to where the "water" is. We, however, must decide to drink. This guide can also lead us to our most compatible spouse, best job and to "pregnant" opportunities. The results are based upon the decisions we make and the actions we take. Once more, freedom of choice can alter any course.

What triggers attraction and love? The trigger varies from person to person. Obviously, hormones play a major part. Additionally, proximity, physical attractiveness, similarity, reciprocity, intimacy and a desire to be with another romantically or sexually. For me, it is beauty and simplicity; for whoever I am attracted to and fall in love with is beautiful and is simple. I am attracted to beauty in people, works of art and nature. Simplicity makes life easier to enjoy. Whatever the reason, we find the one we are attracted to, to be beautiful. Beauty is the greatest trigger for attraction.

Beauty is balance, harmony and radiant energy. It is all the pieces of a puzzle in their proper place. Beauty is felt in the heart and touches the soul. Beauty radiates a special energy that announces itself. Beauty is never a consequence of reason; it is merely felt and experienced. What is beautiful is easy to love, for beauty engenders joy.

There are two kinds of beauty. The naturally beautiful, which is a combination of balance, harmony and radiant energy that announces itself. This beauty is obvious and can be stunning at times. It is a beauty that is shared by many. There is also a second kind of beauty, personal beauty, which is conferred. This beauty is in the eyes of the beholder. This beauty is bestowed by the lover upon the beloved.

The beautiful is always attractive. Seeing something or someone as beautiful the first time is easy. Continuing to do so, however, requires intention, will and effort. It is only natural that repeated exposure and familiarity dull the senses. Overfamiliarity leads to lack of interest and boredom. The human brain is structured to crave new experiences. Newness can be introduced by changing the environment, focusing on a new aspect of the familiar, or by seeing the familiar as if for the first time. This requires effort, intent, and mental discipline.

There are several types of attraction and love, varying from those to individuals, family, nature and God. There is also romantic attraction and love. While human love changes over time, divine love is different. It never diminishes. God's love for us is the only unconditional love. It does not depend on circumstance or our actions, regardless of their nature. We are always loved.

We all have a piece of this divine love within us. We can awaken this love and learn to love others divinely because each of us is a unique reflection of the divine. When we realize others for who they really are, an aspect of the creator, then the fire of divine love is ignited within us and can never be extinguished.

It is easy to love someone we are attracted to as divine. It is much more difficult to do the same for a person we do not get along with. To make it easier for us to see this person differently, we can ask ourselves the following questions:

Who is this person in essence?

Why did this person come into my life and what can I learn through this individual?

How is this person different from me? Can this difference be celebrated?

What can this person teach me?

We all have the exact same origin and destination. There are only two doorways through which we enter and exit earth: birth and death. We germinate on earth as seeds from a fertilized egg. We grow, taking different paths. We share a great deal with each other, and yet we are each unique. Our differences are mostly circumstantial, due to environment, culture, and opportunity.

Being different from each other is not an obstacle to expressing and experiencing divine love. In fact, differences are a revelation of the true nature of Being - diversity. We are diverse, with unlimited modes of expression, all worthy of admiration, marvel, and divine love. Variety is the spice of life. It makes our journey interesting, challenging, and worthwhile.

The Hermetic philosophers taught the adage: "as above, so below" or "the microcosm is a reflection of the macrocosm." Looking at my life, I see the various stages I went through and experienced – a microcosm of diversity. I have been a child - weak, sick, ignorant, destitute, and I have been an adult - mature, powerful, radiantly healthy, confident and prosperous. I love all aspects of me for they make up who I am. Similarly, all of us, with our diversities, add up to the wholeness of humanity. We are all worthy of love.

I love diversity and unique individualities for others have aspects, traits, and skills that I lack and can appreciate and enjoy. I am glad for the marvelous musicians, superb athletes, talented singers, creative dancers, imaginative artists, inspired writers, break-through inventors, and even decent politicians. I admire and appreciate them all. They enrich my life.

I am fully aware that there is a dark side to humanity as well. There are those who rob, commit crimes, lie, cheat, take advantage of others, and abuse. These are also aspects of the divine creator, albeit dark, immature and at an earlier stage of spiritual development. These individuals represent opportunities for us to lend them a helping hand and to contribute to their growth and maturity.

The road to wisdom often winds through ignorance. The dark side highlights the importance of the light, for only light can dispel darkness. We have all been there, on the other side, before we matured. There is a hierarchy of being. Each of us occupies a rung on this helical ladder of life. We reach heaven having occupied all rungs of the ladder. A university student judging an elementary student as ignorant does not understand development and the stages of life. We need each other, for together we are whole and complete.

There are three main reasons we are attracted to and fall in love with another. Our beloved acts as a mirror reflecting and revealing our shortcomings. For it is only through the intimate and constant interaction with another that our hidden defects become obvious. Once exposed, we can work on them.

The second reason we are attracted to and fall in love with another is to share the journey of life and make the trip more pleasurable. Together we can share the ups and downs of life, find imaginative solutions to our challenges and forge opportunities for each other to grow. As we grow, we constantly recreate ourselves.

The final reason we are attracted to and fall in love with another is because the seed of the creator is within us. Since the creator is love, beauty, and joy we are attracted to each other to discover and experience love, beauty, and joy.

INSIGHTS I LIVE BY

The only thing worse than being blind is having sight but no vision.

— *Helen Keller*

P rior to my Near-Death Experience (NDE), I had an irresistible urge to put my "house" in order, write my will, and leave something of value behind for my daughter. I decided that the best legacy I could leave behind was my insights. So I began to write them down. Since I did not die, I continued to develop my insights and ended up with my first book: A Passion for Living, a Path to Meaning and Joy. For more information about my NDE, please refer to my book.

An insight is an accurate and deep intuitive understanding. It is a personal view of the interior workings of something. It is a realization of a truth. As our experiences and knowledge increase, we can have better insights. A person cannot have an engineering insight if that person does not have a background in applied sciences. I have had some amazing insights because of my continuous education since my youth. I have read innumerable books on various subjects, attended many workshops and seminars, and participated in specialized training courses. After graduating with a Bachelor's Degree from the American University of Beirut, I took several advanced courses there. While in the Army, I took some courses at the National Institute of Health (NIH). I have also been teaching and public speaking for over 40 years. In the process, I grew, matured and transformed myself.

Insights are invited guests. We invite them when we think, ponder, wonder and seek. Once I have an insight, my life changes and I live according to that insight. The following are the current insights I live by:

People

Intrinsically, everyone is the same, cut from the same cloth. People appear to be different because each is at a different place along the journey to awakening. All are born, live and die. Our experiences, however, vary based on what we need in order to grow and mature.

When we are born into this world, we are like a seed dropped into soil. The soil and type of seed might vary, but we all seek and attract into our lives whatever we need for our growth. Hence, whatever we face in life – especially challenges – are opportunities for growth. How we face what comes our way depends on where we are on our journey. Everyone has an equal right to be and to decide the pace and manner of their growth, awakening and maturation.

Freedom of Choice

Freedom of choice is the trademark of being human. It is a most precious gift that should be treasured. Not exercising freedom of choice is a lost opportunity to direct the course of our lives. We can use our freedom of choice to highlight our uniqueness. We can also use it to educate ourselves; to free ourselves from superstition, unfounded truths, limiting traditions, bias and prejudice; to learn from any source; to appreciate diversity; to commit to ideals; and to examine what we accept and believe. Most importantly, we can choose to listen to *The Voice Within* and act on its promptings. Freedom of choice is dormant unless it is put to use. We can choose to, not only lift ourselves up, but also aid others along the way. Some of the most important choices we can make are how to use our time and how to relate to others.

Responsibility

Freedom and responsibility are two sides of the same coin. They must always be considered together. There is no freedom without responsibility unless we are asleep and sleepwalking through life. Accepting responsibility is a sure indication of maturity.

All choices engender consequences for which we are responsible and must bear the results. There is no action without reaction, good or bad. Freedom must be balanced with responsibility or else chaos will result. The most important freedom and responsibility we have is in regards to children: whether or not to have them, how many, and how to best care for them.

Victimization

No one has to be a victim unless they agree to it. A person always has a choice. The options might be limited or undesirable, but choices are always available. We can, at any time, act to change the trajectory of our lives and create our own destiny. As children, we follow our parents around. As adults, we live independent lives. We can think for ourselves. We might need guidance once in a while, but we do not need authorities telling us what to believe and how to live our lives. Believing in ourselves, accepting responsibility for our actions, and acting fearlessly dispels all illusions to victimization.

Positive Outlook

It is important to have a positive outlook on life. This, however, is not escapism. It is not just positive thinking, or a passive process of wanting, daydreaming and fantasizing. It is projecting, imprinting the field, knocking at the door of the "still small voice". (1 Kings 19:12 King James Version). It is asking for guidance about what to do, and then doing the work when the inspiration comes. A positive outlook toward life requires that we constantly monitor our thoughts, feelings and actions.

Thoughts, feelings and actions are of two types: those that enhance, energize, and vitalize the body and those that harm and deteriorate the body. Constructive thoughts, positive actions such as exercise, and optimistic feelings such as joy, contentment, gratitude and appreciation produce beneficial secretions. Destructive thoughts, feelings and actions such as addictions, hatred, anger, intolerance, and jealousy produce damaging secretions. We have the power to tip the scale one way or the other by choosing what to think, how to feel and what to do. The quality of our lives is within our control.

For a long period in our lives, hormones govern our biology. They influence our actions, feelings, and emotions. We cannot control our hormones. We can regulate and sublimate these if we so choose by directing their influence into creative expressions.

Diversity

Diversity and variety are the spices of life. They should be welcomed and appreciated. Just as there are immense varieties of fruits and vegetables, there are vast diversities of people. Just as each fruit or vegetable has a distinct feel and taste, each human is unique.

There are great advantages to diverse groups working together harmoniously. Just look at the human body and what it can do because of all the diverse cells, tissues and organs working together to give rise to the miracle that is the human body. When humans emulate the body and learn to work together instead of warring with each other, miracles will begin to occur and earth will transform into a heaven of our own making. An added advantage of diversity is that it makes specialization easier to achieve.

Individuality

Since we all exist on the same planet and share the same atmosphere, we are connected and influence each other. We are our brother's keeper. Individuality is wonderful when used to advance the individual and enhance humanity. It is cancerous when used at the expense of humanity for the mere advancement of the individual. While humanity is the body, each individual is a cell in this body. The health and vitality of the body depends on the cooperation of all cells, tissues, and organs working together for the benefit of the whole body. Even though we appear to be individual, we are part of a much larger humanity living together on earth.

LESSONS LEARNED

A fool thinks himself to be wise, but a wise man knows himself to be a fool.

— *William Shakespeare*

I t would be nice if we learn most of our life lessons early on so the benefits would stretch over the rest of our lives. I remember one lesson I learned in my youth that had a lasting impact on me. One night, I was on my way home from a late movie in Beirut, Lebanon when I heard someone calling me: "Please Mr. could you watch us play? I want you to be the judge if this guy tries to cheat me. It will only take a minute or two."

I stopped, walked back to where the two of them were and offered to help. They were gambling using a pebble and three thimbles. The object was to guess where the pebble was after shuffling the thimbles. The game seemed so simple and profitable. The player kept winning most of the time. He asked me to join in. Believing that I could earn some easy money, I placed my bet. Instantly, I lost my $5.00. Hoping to recover my loss, I placed another $5.00, then $10.00, and then $20.00. Within a minute or two I lost all of money, $80.00. This money was meant to go toward buying books. I was devastated. After I left, I turned back and saw the two guys shaking hands and splitting their profit. Unbeknownst to me, they were partners in crime.

Most of us are governed by greed or fear which are often used by con artists, or even sales people to prey on us to purchase something, or invest. The good news is that once we learn a painful lesson, we never forget it and hopefully, we never repeat the same mistake.

It is human to make mistakes, most of which are through ignorance and because we do not know any better. When our daughters were young, I used to watch the movie "*The Last Unicorn*" several times with them because I enjoyed the movie so much. Years later, when they were grown up, they told me how terrified they were when they watched it. I had no idea. Raising children is not easy, for we have no prior experience. Relationships are difficult because no two are alike. Living can be a challenge. It is something we have to do, because what is the alternative? There are rewards, nevertheless: exquisite moments of intimacy, shared laughter, and pure joy.

Along our journey through life, we pick up some very valuable lessons. It is unfortunate that we cannot pass our experiences on to family members and friends, for each must learn from their own experiences. We cannot grow and mature unless we "eat our own food." No one else can do it for us. Yet we can share some of what we gleaned from having lived so eventfully; and, at the very least, write our experiences down in case someone might benefit.

Life is an educational system. Just as we do not remember everything from our school years, we do not remember all of our life lessons. We do remember a few things, however. What is even more important is that we are more mature after having gone through school and having experienced life lessons. Here are some of the important lessons that I have learned:

The Value of Self-Esteem

It is imperative that we like, even love ourselves. We must think highly of who we are. We are not our possessions, our bodies, or our heritage. Those determine what we have, not who we are. It would be easy to assume that our upbringing and social status determine our self-esteem, but that would be a mistake. Just because we were once a child, poor, weak, and unable to contribute, does not mean that this is how it will always be. We can grow up, become strong, acquire knowledge and contribute. Our lives are not an accident. We are an integral part of the world. We have intrinsic value because of who we are. No one is more or less valuable than another, for each is an essential link in the vast chain of humanity. Some might be better at some skills and abilities, but no one has our exclusive combination of attributes that distinguishes us as a unique expression of God. We are neither above nor below anyone else, for we all possess a divine spark within us. Some appear to be more important or more fortunate than others, but that is only an illusion and is good only for this lifetime. Next lifetime, the tables might be turned and those individuals might be the less fortunate ones. High self-esteem is not something we think about or believe in. We must know in our hearts and being that we matter and that we are valuable.

Learning to accept and value ourselves as unique expressions of the divine is very important to living rich, impactful, and contented lives. We are not a finished product. Through intention, will, and determination, we can improve ourselves and with each achievement and contribution we make, our self-esteem can grow.

We each have people we admire and think highly of like Jesus, the Buddha, George Washington, Lincoln, Martin Luther King, Jr., Einstein and Dr. Salk. These individuals have ancestors, thousands of them. If any of these ancestors were missing, the chain would be broken and our heroes would not have been born. Even if these ancestors were not important themselves, someone very important was born from their seeds. We, too, could be the ancestors of a future hero. Our value is not limited to ourselves, but extends into the future through our offspring.

The Power of Intention

Clear and focused intention is transformative. Clarifying our intentions helps us to navigate life, attract the opportunities we need, reduce wasting of valuable time, and more fully express ourselves.

To clarify our intentions, we can ask ourselves some serious questions:

What do we value most in life?

What, at a minimum, must we accomplish in this lifetime?

Where do we want to make a difference?

What service must we provide to others?

What lessons must we learn?

What fears must we conquer?

What talents, skills and abilities must we develop and express?

Opportunity

Everything we encounter or attract into our lives is an opportunity to polish a trait, learn a skill, or gain mastery over a situation. Opportunities can be as clear as daylight, or they can hide as a challenge, a difficulty, or even a handicap. Some opportunities are thrust upon us, while we must create others through intent and engagement. Opportunity does not knock. We must knock with clear intentions to create our own opportunities.

Reason for Being

We are here on earth to actualize our divine potential. We can do this by engaging in life and continuously improving. Appreciating our experiences helps us make the most of them. Our experiences are the answers to the questions we pose, whether consciously or subconsciously.

The best way to live a happy, healthy, and productive life is to discover an innate passion, develop it, and then use it to serve others. To be happy, we must make others happy. To receive, we must first give. There is a reason for us being here now. We may or may not discover this reason. Regardless, any contribution we make to advance society is a good enough reason for being here.

Consciousness

Our consciousness is not isolated within us. It is connected to and is a part of all consciousness. What we will and intend consciously is like a stone dropped into the ocean of the subconscious. It creates a ripple effect, attracting what it needs to manifest. Time is not a factor in when the manifestation will occur. It will happen at an appropriate time and place. It is our job to ask and persist. Outcomes are beyond our area of control. We are only responsible for doing our part; then we must trust that the manifestation will occur at the opportune time and place. Our motto should be: Thy will be done (the Higher Self), not mine (the ego). The best use of our consciousness is to consciously plant appropriate "seeds" into our subconscious and to use the superconscious to send and receive healing, peaceful, revitalizing and loving energy.

Mistakes

Making mistakes is natural. However, we must endeavor to not repeat our mistakes, but learn from them, be better because of them, and move on. Being in a material body means that we have a lot we can improve upon. Our mistakes provide valuable opportunities to be better. We are not perfect and we will make mistakes. When we do, it is important to make amends and resolve to be better because of them. We are not here to avoid mistakes. We are here to experience, learn, and gain mastery through our mistakes, failures and disappointments. The road to success is often littered with the debris from our failures.

Education

Education can be a game changer. It has had a huge impact on the quality of my life. However, I believe that education is much more than formal schooling and should be continuous. It should also incorporate critical, independent thinking and cover diverse subjects that broaden our perspective. It requires an open mind, eagerness to learn, acceptance of responsibility and reliance upon ourselves to solve problems. Because we are always emulating and being emulated, we are both learning and teaching at the same time. Engaging in life is the best means of acquiring life skills and an impactful education.

Negatives Can Be Positives

I have had many experiences that I initially perceived as disastrous but later realized were blessings in disguise. I would not be where I am if it were not for these seemingly devastating experiences. Here is one simple example that demonstrates this point.

When I was at Fort Dix, N.J. for basic training I was in the Accelerated Platoon. On the last day of training, I failed my weapons assembly test. My assembled weapon was a bit too loose, so I could not graduate. I felt humiliated and devastated. My platoon members graduated, received promotions and moved on. I was left behind, with no graduation or promotion, but with two free weeks to do with as I pleased. I took some tests and, in the process, applied for a new position. As a result of my "failure", I received a new and much more coveted assignment that proved to be the best thing that could have happened to me. My life was dramatically altered, for the better.

We Are Not Alone

Numerous synchronicities traverse the course of my life. I could write a book detailing these occurrences. Anytime in my life when I desperately needed help, help was always there like magic. I have also had several experiences where I knew I was guided and protected from car crashes and other tragedies. There is a silent presence in my life that is unobtrusively watching over me. Anytime I ask, insist or persist, I receive the answer I need. Likewise, anyone who asks, insists or persists, will receive the answer they need. We are not alone. We have never been alone. We have a Higher Self that is always with us. However, due to free choice, we must request the protection we seek before we receive it.

Time is a Most Precious Commodity

Our lives have a limited time span. Our days are numbered. This makes life precious. Living mindlessly or wasting our time on trivia is squandering our most valuable and irreplaceable commodity – time. Having fun is not a waste of time, but spending hours mindlessly watching television is. Time is the great equalizer. Regardless of who we are, we only have 24 hours each day. What sets us apart is what we do with our time. The best investment of our time is to use it to cultivate our minds, enjoy sharing it with loved ones, and spend some of it to create value for others. We can also relax and commune with self, deity, and nature. Most importantly, we must enjoy our brief time as sojourners on this beautiful planet, Earth. Opening our eyes, hearts and minds makes living more enjoyable and more impactful.

SELF-EXAMINATION

I think life is self-examination. Certainly the voyage that one takes.

— *Richard Gere*

It would be tragic indeed if the only growth we experienced was physical. Physical growth is on autopilot. Emotional, mental and spiritual growth, on the other hand, requires an actual pilot at the helm guiding the process. It was Socrates who said, "An unexamined life is not worth living." The most relevant things we can examine in our lives are our habits, beliefs and actions.

Most of our actions are the result of our habits and beliefs. Habits and beliefs are a major component of our internal environment. They affect the quality of our lives. They can influence what "seeds" take root and grow. They can foster weeds. They can also stifle or enhance the growth of beneficial views. Since we have a choice in what habits we form and what we believe in, why not examine them, feed those that empower us, and weed out those that debilitate us?

Habits are like second nature. They form through repetition. It is easy to examine our habits and replace them with better ones. It is more difficult to bring our beliefs to the surface and take a closer look at them. Let us call forth and examine some of these habits, beliefs and actions.

Habits

Habits are shortcuts. Each person has their own unique set of habits that can be called forth and examined. We have some wonderful habits such as brushing and flossing our teeth. We also have some habits that do not serve us. For brevity, here are three habits we should examine and if needed, alter or replace.

1. Listening

Often, we do not hear the person we are conversing with. Our minds are busy preparing a reply. Why not practice attentive listening until the person finishes speaking, then speak clearly, intelligently and to the point?

2. Eating

Often, we eat too quickly. Why not slow down, become aware of the food, masticate completely, savoring every morsel?

3. First Impressions

Instinctively, we form opinions of others, often immediately and inaccurately. Why not resist the impulse to judge a person? Get to know the individual first before forming an opinion of him or her.

Beliefs

Empowering, examined and personally selected beliefs are a power that can move "mountains." Yet, we harbor many beliefs that are demeaning, childish or even contradictory to other beliefs we hold. Some wonderful beliefs are a belief in self, our abilities and potentiality. Here are a few beliefs that we should examine and if needed, alter or replace.

1. Belief In God

If asked: Who created the world and all that is in it? Most would answer: God. If added: And where is God? Most would answer: Everywhere. Let us highlight the word **everywhere** and examine it carefully. If God is everywhere and there are no exceptions, then there can be nothing else. Everything is of God and is God. This includes everything and everyone without exception.

If everything and everyone is of God and is God, then all are equally divine. The knowledge that everything and everyone is holy, a piece and part of God, changes everything, especially our relationship with others, and ourselves.

How do we view God? What are our beliefs regarding God? Will God punish us for being human, prone to error and mistakes? Will we be damned forever for things we did out of ignorance and immaturity? Is God vindictive, jealous and insecure, in the sense that God demands that we obey and worship Him and no one else?

How does God view us? We have various beliefs. What we believe is not right or wrong. It is simply a choice. This choice makes a difference in the quality of our lives. In other words, we have options as to what we believe. The option I choose is that God sees us as His creations and children, as extensions of Himself. I see myself as loved by God. This love is beyond measure: pure, eternal and unconditional. This causes me to have a high regard for myself because of who I am - loved by God, an aspect of God, and imbued with divine nature.

2. Who Are We?

Is Jesus the only Son of God? If yes, then who are we? We are told that we are children of God. If this is true, does that make us equal to Jesus? It does, yet we vary in our degree of awareness, maturity, and understanding. In essence, however, we are all the same. In expression, each person is on a different path and at a different degree of maturity.

3. Sin

Are humans born with "Original Sin?" What exactly is "Original Sin?" Is it the sin of Adam and Eve passed on to us? If so, do we really believe that the God we worship is so mean and vindictive, that He chooses to punish us for something we never did, but supposedly inherited? Can we legally inherit the consequences of our parents' actions, let alone our ancestors' actions? Our justice system does not punish children for their parents' actions. Why do we suppose that God would do so?

Humans impose their nature on God. Instead of internalizing and projecting the image of a loving, creative and miraculous God, we envision a God with our own imperfect human deficiencies: A God who is judgmental, vindictive, and dysfunctional and favors one group over another. We need to wake up to who God is and express ourselves in His Image instead of the other way around.

Organizations often anthropomorphize God in order to have control and dominion over others. By having us believe in original sin, or any sin for that matter, our religious leaders claim the power of absolution and the ability to forgive sins. They can even sell this power over us for gain, which is what happened in the Middle Ages. Rejecting the inheritance of "Original Sin" frees us, enhances our self-esteem, and helps us honor God. Snubbing the concept of sin altogether lessons our burden and frees us. We make mistakes, which is normal, but we do not sin. Rejecting sin aligns us more to our true nature and makes the image we have of God purer.

4. Commandments

How many commandments do Christians have? Not 10, not 5, but only one. We must love: love God, love our neighbor, and love ourselves. Love is an active principle. It must be the core intention of our lives. It must be the principal force behind our actions. Does God really command us to do anything? I doubt it. Commanding is something humans do, not God. I do not believe Christ commanded us to do anything. It does not reflect His nature. His life showed us how to live a life of love and service. He was a living example of what we can be, of our inherent potential. Commands belong to those under the Law, not to ones living in Grace. By emulating Him, we move from being under the Law to living in Grace.

5. Religion

How we live our lives is an expression of our religious beliefs. Religion is not a mere belief. It is active living. What exactly do we know about our religion? Examine yours. Mine is Christianity. What exactly is Christianity? Christ's teachings were outlined in the Sermon on the Mount. Fundamentally, they involve acceptance of all, no judgment, no retaliation, forgiveness, love and service. I believe the fundamental tenets of Christianity are: "to love and to serve." Neither love nor service is mindless. They are based on acting compassionately and empowering others. Love is not blind. It does not condone reprehensible acts or require us to look the other way. To love is simply to recognize that everyone is an aspect of divinity. Each person is a temple that houses God within. To love also means that individuals are at different stages of awakening. They need our example and support, not our condemnation. Each individual has the same divine potential as everyone else. Each has the right to live as they choose, as long as no one is harmed in the process.

6. Heaven And Hell

Is there a heaven and a hell? Reward and punishment are human qualities, not those of a divine God. God is pure love. Love does not punish. Love is a reward in itself. We are allowed to chart our own path to learn and become enlightened. Living without fear enables us to create the rewards that are personally meaningful for us and to reap the consequences of our actions.

If there is a hell, are we to suppose that all criminals, regardless of the severity of their crimes, are treated the same? Do all "sinners" go to the same place, regardless of the cruelty of their actions? Is the punishment forever – eternal – for things done temporally and in ignorance?

If there is a heaven, is it the same reward for everyone, regardless of the degree of their goodness? Is this fair? Is this just? Additionally, what constitutes heaven? Is it what everyone desires, which varies from one person to the next? Or is it a fanciful creation based upon human hope?

Humans, through their freedom of choice, have created many hells on earth. They can, with the same freedom of choice and intent, transform earth into a heaven of their choosing. We are forged in the image of God; therefore, we are all creators. What we choose to create is entirely up to us. We fashion our own heaven or hell.

7. Soul

What is soul? How do we know that we have a soul? We do not have a soul. We are the soul. The soul is unseen, yet the implications and handiwork of the soul are everywhere. The soul is our identity and eternal essence. The soul is our light and our consciousness. It is the spark of divinity within.

Actions

Finally, we should examine our actions. Often, when people are on one side they grieve and complain. Yet, as soon as they move to the other side, they dish out to others what they were complaining about. We should not do to others what we do not want them to do to us. Hypocrisy is a sign of childishness and immaturity. A good question to ask ourselves is: have I been a hypocrite?

We are at different stages of our lives occupying various positions. If we are **an employee**, here are a few questions to consider:

Have I given my best to the position I occupy?

Have I gone beyond the expected to contribute toward the success of my employer? Have I served our customers to the best of my ability?

If we are **the manager**, or the boss, here are a few questions to consider:

Have I been fair, just and compassionate in my dealings with everyone?

Have I been prejudiced, biased, or discriminatory toward anyone?

Have I used my position to take advantage of anyone?

Have I done my part to encourage the development of my employees?

If we are **not working**, we can still examine our

actions as a human being. Here are a few questions to consider:

Have I taken advantage of anyone? Abused, or mistreated anyone?

Have I caused pain and suffering for anyone?

Have I carried out my duties as a citizen and served my family, community and country the best I am capable of?

Judgement Day is not after we die. The Hall of Justice is our own hearts. We need to enter it regularly and expose ourselves to ourselves. We should weigh our actions against the "feather" of truth, justice and purity. We can pass our own judgment. We are the judge and the jury. It is our lives that we are examining. Self-examination is how we make our soul pure.

QUESTIONS TO CONSIDER

Learn from yesterday, live for today, hope for to-morrow. The important thing is not to stop questioning.

— *Albert Einstein*

One summer when I was young, my Aunt sent me to a Presbyterian Youth Camp. The hope was to indoctrinate me with their teachings. The group was discussing "loving our enemies." After listening to several points of view, I raised my hand to ask a question (in jest): "since I do not have any enemies, is it OK for me to love God's enemy, Satan or the Devil?

Generally, we are not encouraged to question. We are groomed to accept and follow. We are told "Don't rock the boat," "fit in". But when our right to know the truth is at stake, we must question. Asking is the best way we can find answers. We must not ask superficially, however, but rather ask honestly, inquisitively, and persistently until the truth is revealed. So, here are some questions to consider:

How Did Life Start?

According to Biogenesis, life can only proceed from life. How did the first cell come about? From mere chemicals? How can life, an incredibly orderly and interdependent event, spring forth merely as a result of chance? Was the transformation of dead chemicals into living matter the result of random events? I do not believe so. Life did not simply happen. Life and its evolutionary processes are intentional, purposeful, and directed toward ever increasing complexity, efficiency and powerful abilities. Evolution is not mindless. It is intelligently directed by consciousness.

I absolutely believe in evolution. I do not believe in the creation story of humans as stated in the Old Testament. However, I do believe that something unusual happened to the human species some 200,000 years ago that fast-tracked our evolution. There are Mesopotamian records that speak to such an event. The references indicate an enhancement to our species, rather than the creation of a new one.

Highly Sophisticated Compounds

As an electron microscopist, I used to spend lots of time studying cellular components and structures. I was intrigued by the cellular membrane. It is double layered with pores of specific sizes and composition to permit only certain chemicals in and out of the cell. How is this possible merely due to chance? Similarly, how could incredibly complicated compounds, such as DNA, RNA, chlorophyll and hemoglobin form by chance? Can chance and the laws of nature coexist? Science advocates that disorder in the universe is constantly increasing, due to entropy. This is the second law of thermodynamics. However, science ignores that there is another force to counterbalance entropy: Life. Life creates order out of disorder. Living organisms combine and convert the simple into the more organized. Order and organization are the trademark of life, yet science contends that life, order and complicated compounds arose by chance. How can disorder result in incredibly complicated order? My answer is that **if we do not know, then we must keep an open mind until we do.** I believe that consciousness directs order and organization.

Marvels of Engineering

How could metamorphosis, an incredibly intricate process, take place by chance? Imagine the stages a caterpillar has to go through to become a butterfly. The egg becomes a larva, then a chrysalis and finally a butterfly. Similarly, how did it happen that a spider "learned" how to spin a web to trap and catch its prey? How did birds "learn" to build nests? How did they "learn" how and when to migrate? How did bees "learn" to build hives? Can instinct explain these? I know that DNA controls these processes. But how did this information get into the DNA in the first place? Through chance and random mutations? Is it possible for chaos to give rise to extremely sophisticated processes? How did the first egg or the first seed form? Through chance?

How convenient that everything had to be just right for life to start and for evolution to commence? When there are too many coincidences, perhaps it is no longer a coincidence. If we do not know the answer to a puzzle, why not keep an open mind until we do? Once again, I believe that consciousness is the driving force behind these complicated processes.

The Amazing Cell

A cell is like a city. It has factories with assembly lines that generate energy. It has an extensive communications system. It can defend, heal, exchange carbon dioxide for oxygen and expel waste. It monitors what come in and what goes out. It is a highly elaborate and complicated system.

How did the initial cell form? How did a cell learn how to divide? Cell division is the way life perpetuates and avoids extinction. Cell division implies a pre-existing knowledge of an upcoming death. Replicating the entire genome sequence is unimaginably complicated. Could this have happened by chance? Obviously, to accidentally learn to replicate would require an enormous amount of trial and error, which would theoretically consume an inordinate amount of time. Failure would mean a fresh start for life. So, how did cell division come about? By accident, or does consciousness direct all life events? I understand that just because we do not have answers today does not mean that we will never have the answers we seek. Yet, we know that living beings respond to changes in the environment and this response to the changes in the environment is driving evolution. Living beings are imbued with consciousness. Is consciousness the active force behind evolution?

Survival

If survival is the primary urge of life, why do we die? If the traits that survive in a species are the ones that aid our survival on the planet, why haven't we evolved a trait that prevents our death? Why do we still succumb to old age and the ravages of disease? Enough time has passed since the start of life for evolution to grant us physical perfection and immortality. Why hasn't this manifested? Where are the random forces of evolution that would make this happen? Is the life cycle of birth, growth, and death necessary? If so, why? If survival of our species is a priority, why have we not established peaceful coexistence, so that our species has a better chance to survive? We have mostly been a warring species. We have killed millions of our own. Even though our minds are highly evolved, we use our minds for creativity and destruction, often for creative destruction. Is it possible that we are growing, learning and maturing rather than simply, randomly, evolving?

Devolution

We are not the best at everything. We have used our opposable thumbs to make tools that are more sophisticated than other animals. We learned how to use fire to cook and generate warmth. We also learned to use language to convey information about danger, poisonous foods, etc. Our physical abilities, on the other hand, are not the most evolved. Many animals have better eyesight, keener hearing, faster speed, more powerful strength, and a more acute sense of smell. Some say that we had to give up these abilities to develop our brains. But we could have both highly developed brains and highly evolved senses and abilities. Why hasn't this happened? Why did some of our abilities regress? Why do our teeth decay, our eyesight degenerate and our muscles atrophy with age? Why would evolution allow us to degrade? Is it possible that struggle and shortcomings are necessary aspects of growth and maturity?

Inspiration

What is the nature of inspiration? How does it happen? Inspiration births new ideas, but where do these new ideas come from? I have personally experienced inspiration on numerous occasions. In fact, most of my writing is inspired. I am as amazed as anyone else as to what I have written. The way it works for me is that I ask, I persist, and I wait for the answer to appear.

Jesus said: "Ask, and it will be given to you; seek, and you will find; knock, and it will be opened to you. For everyone who asks receives, and the one who seeks finds, and to the one who knocks it will be opened."   *Mat. 7:7-8*

Ask, Seek, Knock. These are active verbs. We must ask and persist. We must seek until we find. We must knock until we are heard and the door opens. We must invite and anticipate inspiration.

Where do our new ideas come from? We can receive inspiration from others, but mostly inspiration comes from the overall consciousness surrounding us. As we ask, seek, and knock, we attract the answers we need. Keep in mind that we are immersed in consciousness and connected to the source of inspiration. To receive, however, we cannot simply ask, seek and knock. We must insist and persist, even demand answers. We must be intentional and know that we are deserving of those answers.

Prometheus was a champion of mankind in Greek mythology; he stole fire from the gods and gave it to mortals. I understand Prometheus as an archetype for inspiration. We receive the fire of the gods anytime we are inspired.

Knowing

Knowing is similar to inspiration in that it just happens. We simply know as if from out of the blue. Knowing is different from reasoning and understanding. It is instantaneous. It lands on us and engulfs us. We simply know. All the pieces of the puzzle come together and a picture emerges.

I have experienced several intuitive "knowings." I have known what is going to happen before it happens. I have known what to do at critical junctures in my life. I have also known where to live, which house to buy, and even whom to marry.

One of the most profound "knowings" that I have had was the crystal-clear knowledge that I was about to die. Over the course of a few days, I had my Near-Death Experience. That experience was transformational. For a detailed description of this event, please refer to my book: *A Passion for Living, a Path to Meaning and Joy.*

Last night I had a dream. I was in a classroom with several students I do not know. The one sitting to my left had a project he was working on. I knew all about his project, even his last test grade, without being told. I simply knew. How? I do not know.

We should examine our lives for instances when we knew, simply, clearly, and beyond any shadow of a doubt. Perhaps investigating "knowing" will open up new doorways for insights and opportunities to get to know ourselves and others more profoundly. Above all, we should never cease questioning.

AGING

You can free yourself from aging by reinterpreting your body and by grasping the link between belief and biology.

— *Deepak Chopra*

It is interesting how the way we look at ourselves is different from the way others see us. We have a self-image that does not change much over the years. We have the impression that we are always the same. Even though I am in my early seventies, because I am in excellent health, I do not see myself as a senior citizen. How others see me, however, is a different story. One day, a few years back, I went to a Burger King for a Whopper. The bill was less than what I expected. When I asked the server for the reason, she told me that she gave me a 10% senior citizen discount. I was shocked. I did not know that I looked that old. Another time this happened was when we were in Egypt. While addressing our guide in Arabic, I referred to him as my brother. He, in turn, referred to me as his uncle. I was shocked once more. I thought we were the same age.

Why We Age?

We seem to follow the bell curve. We are born, grow up, peak, and then begin to decline. The law of entropy takes hold. The second law of thermodynamics states that entropy always increases with time. Entropy is lack of order, a gradual decline into disorder; for the body, it is aging.

A second reason we age is because we have a biological clock that keeps track of time and ensures our aging. Our cells are programmed to divide a certain number of times (between 50 and 70) and then cease dividing. With each cell division, the telomeres shorten and once they get too short, cells can no longer divide. *(Telomeres are protective caps at the ends of chromosomes that become shorter with each cell division.)*

A third reason we age is due to accumulation. We are constantly accumulating days (time), experiences, and the memories and emotions from these experiences. Some of these are beneficial, but most are not. Over time, most of what we accumulate turns into rubble. Accumulation leads to added weight that drags and slows us down. If life is a flow, the debris we accumulate becomes a sludge which restricts our movement, hinders the flow of life, and causes rigidity, aging, and eventual death.

A fourth contributor to aging is what is known as Original Sin in Christianity, or what is known as karma in Hinduism and Buddhism. These are embedded, debilitating memories of experiences we are born with or inherit. The impact of these are toxins, often manifesting as anger, guilt, shame, and even physical defects. These hasten the aging of the body.

What Can We Do About It?

A. Slowing It Down

We cannot stop aging, but we can slow it down. We can also make the most of our time. A day can be wasted or it can be savored. Life is a measure of days lived, not just counted. Here are a few things we can do to slow down aging and make the most of our time.

1. Excitement about life is essential. Excitement can be about a job, a project, a grandchild, or anything else. Excitement and savoring time spent with loved ones is especially beneficial.

2. Having a positive outlook and expectation makes a difference in our energy level and our ability to enjoy our activities.

3. Being in love and caring deeply about a person, project, or activity.

4. Being alive to beauty in people and in nature.

5. Having a high regard for self.

6. Communing with the body, and imprinting it with images of youth, vigor and vitality.

7. Avoiding boredom, stagnation, and resignation.

8. Keeping an open mind, remaining flexible and becoming child-like, playful, inquisitive and curious.

9. Nurturing the body, avoiding destructive addictions and exercising.

10. Remaining flexible.

The difference between the young and the aged is their degree of flexibility, adaptability, curiosity, interest, and enthusiasm. The aged have mostly lost their flexibility, adaptability, interest, passion and curiosity. The young have a lightness of being. The aged are burdened with boring jobs, unwelcome responsibilities, and debilitating diseases. While the young are full of vitality, the aged become depleted. While the young have a lot to look forward to, the aged do not want to prolong their misery. They give up, age and slowly die.

We can change all that. We can become like children again. We can rekindle our interest, passion and curiosity. We can remain flexible and adaptable. We can find and engage in exciting jobs. If we can't do that, then we can pretend that our jobs are interesting and that we are making a valuable contribution. If we cannot do that, we can engage in an all-together different activity, or even look for a new job. We can also assume our responsibilities with joy and gratitude. Health, vitality, and vigor are results of several factors. Among them are heredity and genes, hormones, and a cocktail of contributors to health. These are: diet and nutrition, including what to eat, how much, when and in what combinations; exercise and stimulation; rest and sleep; cleanliness and proper elimination; positive mental, emotional and spiritual frameworks; sunshine; entertainment, hobbies, and interests; joyful communion, laughter, play, and having fun; social engagements and fulfilling sex. This is a long list and can be confusing. To keep it simple, all we need to do is desire health, assume responsibility for our bodies, use common sense, and listen to *The Voice Within* for guidance.

B. Programming

Our bodies are constantly changing. We are never the same from moment to moment. Our cells divide and regenerate a new version of us every few years. Why does this process stop? Where did the programming in our cells come from? If it is in our DNA, how did it get there? If we are primed and programmed for survival, why do we age and die?

The good news is that all programs can be reprogrammed, altered, modified and improved upon. It is highly probable that our cellular programming came from our environment. We can access this program and influence it in ways we choose. We can do this for three reasons:

1. We have constantly been programmed, ever since we were born. Imitating our parents is the beginning of our programming. Self-programming continues throughout our lives, decreasing with old age. If we can be programmed, then we can also be re-programmed; but this time, by us, with the intent to live healthier and longer.

2. If we can shorten our lives through harmful behaviors, such as poor nutrition, lack of exercise, smoking and drug abuse, we must be able to influence the body in a positive way to lengthen our lives. We have mental tools that we can employ to combat aging. These are visualization, self-talk with clarity and intent, and specific exercises, such as cleansing and releasing. We can commune with our body parts at the cellular level, knowing that our cells respond to pictures and intentions. Since we energize whatever we dwell on, we should visualize ourselves as our best self. This helps re-program and imprint our cells with what we want.

3. Medical science has demonstrated that expectations play a major role in how we heal and recover from disease. Expectation can also get us sick. What we expect with confidence plays a role in the shortening or lengthening of our lives.

We are always programming ourselves, although we do not know it. Seeing others age, get sick and die, programs us. Education is a form of programming. So is self-talk. Additionally, when we visualize, imagine and meditate, we are influencing our bodies. It is best to take control and impact the body, consciously and in the manner we want. Here is how to do it.

First, we must realize that **we are the boss**, that our bodies **are our factories** and that our cells **are our employees**. We can "speak" to our "employees" and they will listen and comply. Like a good boss, it is best to first praise the employees for the excellent job they have been doing. Then tell them what you want: health, vitality and rejuvenation. Your request must be clear, loving and emphatic. You are the boss. Visualize what you want. Only state what you desire, never how it should be carried out or when it should be done by. Trust your employees to do their job. They are the best in the business. They have been taking care of you for a long time. They know what they are doing. Here are a few of the things your employees constantly do for you: they repair your injuries, keep you healthy and heal you from sickness, digest food for you, give you energy, eliminate waste and reproduce new cells. Take good care of them and they will take care of you. They are invaluable.

C. Accumulation

To remain young, we must de-junk! We must replace depressing emotions with uplifting ones. We must continuously weed the undesirable impacts and feed the desirables! If we remain light, we stay young. Most first experiences are exciting, exhilarating and joyous. Like the first time we are in love, see snow, visit an exotic place or taste an especially delicious food. Over time and with repetition, even our best experiences lose their luster, and become routine and dull. To maintain our excitement and to prevent our joyous experiences from becoming burdensome, we can train ourselves to see with fresh eyes. We can pretend that we are seeing and experiencing things as if for the first time. We can remain curious, marvel at, celebrate, and enjoy the simple wonders around us. Fortunately for us, we live on an incredibly beautiful planet. It is a Garden of Eden. What we need are eyes that see and appreciate the diversity and beauty that surrounds us.

There are two kinds of memories that we normally accumulate: sad, heavy, negative memories that drag us down and light, joyous memories that lift us up. Since we can, why not drop the negative ones and hold onto the joyous ones? We can eliminate our negative memories by releasing or sublimating them. At the same time, we can add to our uplifting memories by experiencing simple pleasures: communing with self, others and nature; loving, appreciating, wondering, expressing creativity, and enjoying intimacy. These will create uplifting, light, and invigorating memories. These memories will keep us young, and heal and rejuvenate us.

When we experience sad and tragic events, we can let their memory be temporary. We do not have to store them permanently or continue to dwell on them. We can experience them, release them, and move on.

We cannot simply delete bad memories. We can, however, replace them. Here is a simple exercise we can undertake to rejuvenate, revitalize, slow down or reverse our aging. While in the shower, as we are using water to wash ourselves, we can visualize that the water is washing away any traumatic memories and accumulated debris. We can also invite uplifting, positive and joyous energies and memories to replace the ones that we just washed away. We can imagine that the water is baptizing us and we are becoming new, vital, energetic, and youthful. We can do this every time we shower. We can also inhale invigorating energy and exhale the debris.

D. Releasing/Letting Go/Forgiveness

There are two references in Christianity to releasing and letting go of what is known as sin or Karma. One is baptism and the other is forgiveness. Baptism is where our "sins" are washed away, while the value of forgiveness is gleaned from a story in Luke 5:18-26

And behold, some men were bringing on a bed a man who was paralyzed, and they were seeking to bring him in and lay him before Jesus, but finding no way to bring him in, because of the crowd, they went up on the roof and let him down with his bed through the tiles into the midst before Jesus. And when he saw their faith, he said, "Man, your sins are forgiven you." And the scribes and the Pharisees began to question, saying, "Who is this who speaks blasphemies? Who can forgive sins but God alone?" When Jesus perceived their thoughts, he answered them, "Why do you question in your hearts? Which is easier, to say, 'Your sins are forgiven you,' or to say, 'Rise and walk'? But that you may know that the Son of Man has authority on earth to forgive sins" —he said to the man who was paralyzed— "I say to you, rise, pick up your bed and go home." And immediately he rose up before them and picked up what he had been lying on and went home, glorifying God. And amazement seized them all, and they glorified God and were filled with awe, saying, "We have seen extraordinary things today."

Unless we intentionally work at letting go of these burdens, they will age us prematurely. We can let go, not only of our "Original Sin", or Karma, but also of our current "sins" of commission or omission by practicing forgiveness - forgiveness of ourselves and others. By letting go, we become lighter, rejuvenated, and we live longer.

My aim is not to live as long as I possibly can, but rather to see all that I want to see, spend enough time with those I value, do all that I desire to undertake, experience all that I decide on, and create happy memories, while living with health and vitality.

LIFE AND DEATH

A teacher at the private Head-Royce School in Oakland, CA. asked his students: "I am the beginning of everything, the end of everywhere. I am the beginning of eternity, the end of time and space. What am I?"

—*As reported in* The Washington Post
12/30/2019

The first guess from a first grader was "death". The answer, however, is the letter "e". Why we die is a mystery. Life has been evolving on planet Earth for billions of years. If the struggle for survival is an evolutionary fact, why then do we not survive as individuals? Science would say that survival is for the species, not the individual. However, the vast majority of species that ever existed have long been extinct.

Why didn't the cell, and the tissues, organs, and systems along with it, find a way to perpetuate the body and make the individual immortal? This is not as difficult as it seems. If the cells found a way to be alive, why not keep on living? In fact, it is far more difficult to master cell replication than to perpetuate life. Imagine learning how to duplicate the entire genetic code, about three billion nucleotides, flawlessly, in order for the cell to divide. This is indeed a Herculean achievement. Additionally, manufacturing DNA, RNA, hemoglobin, and chlorophyll are more difficult to achieve than perpetuating life.

Is it possible that the body did, in fact, learn not to die? Even though the cells die by the thousands, the body continues on living. Perhaps there are two kinds of immortality:

1. Physical immortality: Continuing to live in the same body forever.

2. Cyclic immortality: Living forever, but in different bodies, one in each lifetime. The individual continues to live forever, as soul, incarnating in a new body each time.

Obviously, the preferred choice is reincarnation. For it is of no use to have immortality in the same body as long as the body continues to age and atrophy. We tend to forget that the body, without consciousness, is inert and lifeless. The body has no power of volition on its own. The body is the chariot, while consciousness is the charioteer. The body is the vehicle, while consciousness is the driver. Keeping this in mind, it is absolutely possible that, to overcome the ravages of disease and aging, consciousness, ingeniously, came up with cyclic immortality via reincarnation.

Cyclic immortality, or reincarnation, has incredible advantages over singular body immortality. Here are a few:

1. Each rebirth is a fresh start in a new body.

2. Each life starts with a new family, under novel environments, allowing the individual to have innovative experiences and hence alleviate boredom.

3. The brain and the mind never get dull from the continuous accumulation of memories and experiences. With the start of each cycle, the slate is wiped clean.

4. The lessons learned from our experiences are carried over from one lifetime to another as aspects of character and personality.

5. Growth, learning, maturation, and awakening can continue indefinitely.

6. Boredom and death are conquered.

7. Exciting new encounters with different people, new spouses and children are enjoyed.

8. Over several lifetimes, human actions can experience their consequences, karma is fulfilled, and justice is served.

9. We start each life oblivious to the fact that we have lived before. This is important because it makes our lives precious, for each comes with an expiration date.

10. By making each life terminal, with a fixed duration, we have the impetus and the incentive to accomplish the most within the allotted timeframe. If we were in the same body eternally, then our incentive to perform would diminish.

11. Finally, cyclic immortality explains why we age, why our faculties atrophy and why we suffer. What matters most for eternal beings are combatting loss of interest, lack of curiosity and a nonchalant attitude toward living. Hence, a variety of experiences, regardless of their nature, is of the utmost importance.

12. By having lived in various bodies, in different countries, and with diverse cultures, we become broad-minded, grow and mature, and have an opportunity to appreciate our planet even more.

It is difficult to imagine that the body can come up with such an ingenious plan to perpetuate its existence. Reincarnation is an inventive strategy indeed, and it is hard to believe that it can be true. However, once we realize that life is conscious and that, in fact, consciousness is in charge, is the planner, and is the driving force behind evolution, then it is easy to accept that such a plan can indeed be devised and is, in fact, operational. Perhaps death is not a deficiency of nature. Individual death might even be due to choice, albeit, a subconscious choice. For more information as to why we choose to die, please refer to my book: **A Passion for Living, a Path to Meaning and Joy**.

> *Only Almitra was silent, gazing after the ship until it had vanished into the mist. And when all the people were dispersed, she still stood alone upon the sea-wall, remembering in her heart his saying: "A little while, a moment of rest upon the wind, and another woman shall bear me."*
>
> *Kahlil Gibran, The Prophet*

MYSTERY OF DREAMS

Hold fast to dreams, for if dreams die, life is a broken-winged bird that cannot fly.

—Langston Hughes

The ancients relied heavily on dreams and dream interpretations. Ancient cultures and religions are full of instances where messages were received in a dream and were taken seriously. Here are two instances:

But God came to Abimelech in a dream by night and said to him, "Behold, you are a dead man because of the woman whom you have taken, for she is a man's wife." Gen 20:3

Now the birth of Jesus Christ took place in this way. When his mother Mary had been betrothed to Joseph, before they came together she was found to be with child from the Holy Spirit. And her husband Joseph, being a just man and unwilling to put her to shame, resolved to divorce her quietly. But as he considered these things, behold, an angel of the Lord appeared to him in a dream, saying, "Joseph, son of David, do not fear to take Mary as your wife, for that

which is conceived in her is from the Holy Spirit.
Matt 1:18-20

Dreams are "picture thoughts." The same way that thoughts appear as a result of involuntary stimulation, dreams happen for the same reason. Thoughts and dreams are responses to stimuli. It is said that dreams are projections of the mind and are not real. Some say that we dream as a way for the brain to reorganize itself based on our daily experiences. Others contend that we dream to resolve issues or that our dreams can even be influenced by the food we eat or the drugs we consume. Finally, concerns, worries and pressing issues can also induce our dreams.

These explanations are helpful, but unsatisfactory in explaining the intricate nature of dreams. We dream a multitude of dreams every night with diverse themes and degrees of sophistication. Some dreams are very detailed, complex, and unusual. I have had many dreams with diverse themes in a single night. I have dreamt of people that I have absolutely no idea who they are. I have also had prophetic dreams in which I experience the content of my dream the very next day. So, there must be more to dreams than is first apparent. Dreams are transient and we only remember portions of dreams, and for a very short time, if we remember them at all. Of what use are dreams if we cannot hold onto them or barely remember them? Even though most dreams are effervescent, bubbling up momentarily and then gone and forgotten forever, some dreams are vivid, impactful and unforgettable. Why? I remember a dream I had in the early 1960s when I was in the monastery in Lebanon. That dream was transformative. The details in that dream were far better than my waking reality. Hence, not all dreams are the same. We cannot lump them into one category.

I believe that we dream for at least five fundamental reasons:

1. Reflection Of Our Dual Nature

We dream to reflect our dual nature. We exist in a multi-verse and are not confined to the body. Our reality transcends the physical. We are multi-dimensional and we function on multiple levels concurrently. We are consciousness. Consciousness is energy. Energy manifests in infinite forms. So do we. We might believe that we are limited to the physical body. We are not. We are a soul in a physical body. We live two lives: a physical life, in four-dimensional space/time governed by the laws of nature, and a spiritual life, in the higher dimensions not governed by space or time. In our daily lives, we move from point A to point B. It takes time. We use language to communicate with others. Gravity controls our movements. We are confined and limited. Not so when we are dreaming.

Dreams are multi-dimensional. Often, they do not make sense because they are symbolic and not literal. At times, they are very meaningful and can provide us with solutions to issues we are concerned about. They can also inspire us. They are a reflection of our true nature, the soul, which is free, unencumbered, creative and multi-dimensional. Dreams are captured frames of the immense activities of the soul. Being non-physical, our soul can be in many places and participate in many activities at once. Once we wake up, we become, once again, confined to the laws and restrictions of the physical world.

Sleep, dreams and wakefulness are a reflection of our deeper reality. While living, we are awake. When we die, we enter the sleep and dream state. Are sleep, dreams and wakefulness a reflection of reincarnation and our cyclic existence? Just as in the same night we might sleep and wake up several times, so it is with the cycles of life and reincarnation. Sometimes we sleep for a few hours and then remain awake for a long time. Other times, we sleep for a long time and are awake for a short time. In an analogous way, sometimes we live long lives and do not reincarnate for a long time, and other times we live short lives and reincarnate soon after. Will we continue to repeat the cycles of sleep and wakefulness, undergoing reincarnations, until we are finally fully awake?

2. Life Is A Dream

> "...now your whole life, from birth unto death, with all its dreams, is it not in its turn also a dream, which we take as the real life, the reality of which we do not doubt only because we do not know of the other more real life?"
>
> Leo Tolstoy quoted by Shirley MacLaine in: Out on a Limb

Parents often tell their children who wake up from a dream afraid, that it is "only a dream", which implies that dreams are not real. While dreaming, a dream is very real for the dreamer. We do not know that we are dreaming until we wake up.

The same is true for when we are supposedly awake. We do not know that, in fact, we are in a dream state until or unless we are forced to fully wake up due to an intense experience or a trauma. The law of inertia applies. We continue to sleepwalk through life until we are jolted into wakefulness. Perhaps the reason we continue to sleep and dream is a reminder that we can be fooled into believing that we are awake when we are not or, that we are, at best, only partially awake. That is why Adam and Eve were naked and did not realize it. They were asleep and did not know it until their eyes were opened due to a unique experience.

Christ said: "We have eyes but cannot see, ears but cannot hear." (Matt 8:18). Perhaps this is because we are trapped in a dream state, believing that we are awake. We are lulled into sleep by our limiting beliefs, fears, superstitions, and ignorance.

The significant difference between dream and wakeful reality is that while awake, we can exercise our freedom of choice; choose and act consciously. We are awake when we exercise conscious control over our thoughts, feelings and actions. We are awake when we employ our intentions and take purposeful actions. Otherwise, we are asleep, taken over by forces beyond our control, victims of circumstance. **Freedom of choice can only matter when we learn to use it.** Unless we exercise our freedom of choice and decide, we are asleep. When we do, we are awake.

Row, row, row your boat
Gently down the stream
Merrily, merrily, merrily, merrily
Life is but a dream

Life is but a dream. A dream is an experience. We experience in order to wake up to our true nature - creative and magnificent beings. How awake or asleep we are is a matter of degree. It is, however, entirely up to us. We can sleepwalk through life, or we can wake up, take the helm, and direct the course of our journey. Once again, it is totally up to us.

3. We Are Creative

Daydreams are conscious projections of things we want to do or achieve. Could it be that night dreams are subconscious projections of things we want to do or achieve? I believe so. We dream because we are creative. The mind continues to create reflecting its innate nature, creativity. One of the easiest forms of creativity is putting together various parts in new combinations and sequences. We do this in our dreams. A critical fact to remember is that we are the authors of our dreams, the creators of all of the actors in our dreams. We are powerful creators. To create, we must first dream. The catalysts for our creativity are needs, desires and pressing issues. We create best using our imagination. Dreaming is an involuntary use of our imagination.

During my first evening in the U.S., Monday, February 14, 1972, my family introduced me to the show,

I Dream of Jeannie. Barbara Eden was the Genie in that show. She could instantly grant wishes and make dreams come true. We, too, have a Genie within us. It is a combination of mind, heart, inspiration and *The Voice Within.* To access our Genie requires pure intention, focused attention and fearless action. If we learn to "rub" these into wakefulness, they too can grant us any wish and make our dreams come true.

4. Dreams As Communications From Our Higher Self

I have had a few spiritual dreams. I have had dreams where I was in class learning important spiritual lessons. I have also had dreams in which I was in council with spiritual personalities, observing and learning. And I have had several recurring dreams which were communications from my Higher Self. One particular recurring dream was persistent over several years. However, due to the symbolic nature of the dream, I did not understand the meaning of those dreams until many years later when the meaning became crystal clear, but by then I could not prevent the manifestation that my Higher Self was warning me about.

I have also, on several occasions, woken up from sleep and dreams with answers to questions that I had been dwelling on. I have had many breakthrough insights after waking up from a dream.

5. Dreams Prepare Us For Transition (Death)

My personal favorite reason for why we dream is, perhaps, because it prepares us for transition – death. We are going to die and fear of the unknown might prompt us to hold on for dear life. We might not let go voluntarily. Having dreamt millions of dreams and remembering some of them, a few vividly, allows our subconscious to relax in the knowledge that perhaps death is not a finality. Dreaming of dead relatives makes that even clearer. Seeing dead relatives in dreams might indicate that they are alive in spirit, a comforting thought indeed.

As we get older, dreams become sweet escapes. We yearn for beautiful dreams. Believing that the afterlife must be analogous to sleep time, we let go. We pass to the other side hoping that what was dreams on this side of life becomes reality on the other side.

Food for Thought

The ancient Hermetics advocated the adage: as above, so below. This is in reference to the law of correspondence and can be variously stated as: as within, so without; as the universe, so the soul; or as on earth so in heaven. There is a great deal of correspondence between dreams and wakeful living – two sides of the same coin.

1. Dreams are projections of the mind where we represent events to ourselves and we react to these representations. Does this hold true in our wakeful world as well?

2. Our dreams are OUR dreams. We are the creators, authors, directors, and all the actors in our dreams.

Forgetting this fact, we can choose to be a mere figure in our own dreams. Does this hold true in our wakeful world as well?

3. Reality is fluid in dreams. We only remember what we want and need to remember. After a while, most fade away from memory. Does this hold true in our wakeful world as well?

4. Dreams appear real and we react to them. We only know that they were mere dreams after we wake up. Does this hold true in our wakeful world as well?

5. While asleep, we enter and leave a dream without any awareness of a "before" or an "after" to the dream. We have no knowledge of what came before the dream began, or what happens after we exit the dream. We are born and we die without any knowledge of a "before" birth or an "after" to living.

6. Dreams appear to take place in space/time. In fact, they only occur in the mind. Does this hold true in our wakeful world as well? Where do our experiences take place? Is space/time a mere projection of mind?

7. How do we see, hear and communicate in a dream? Our eyes are closed and our senses are asleep. Mostly non-verbal communication takes place in a dream. How? Do we communicate non-verbally in wakeful life and are not aware of it?

8. How can we dream of people, in great detail, when in wakeful life we cannot remember many of the details? My mind paints and projects people that in wakeful life I can never draw. How can dreams access details that I, consciously, cannot?

9. Dreams are projections of the mind. They do not endure. This is because their source is a mind in its infancy. Just as the baby dragons in The Game of Thrones could not spew fire until they grew up, so it is with mind. Once fully developed, a powerful mind can project detailed, vivid, colorful and lively thought forms that ally with other thought forms and create more enduring realities. Is this how the universe and all that is in it came about? Perhaps.

10. Dreaming is an innate ability. However, dreams are mostly random, uncontrolled mental projections. Once we develop the ability to consciously control and project these "dreams", we create and experience what we want, instead of the random and haphazard experiences we are now having. We become conscious creators.

UNSEEN

Dark matter is one of the dominant constitu-
ents of the universe, which piled up in certain
parts of the universe due to gravity, and in those
regions, galaxies were formed. It is the unseen
thing that holds the universe together.

— *Priyamvada Natarajan*

M ost of us have our usual five senses. Some are
blind and cannot see. Others are deaf and cannot hear. Those of us who have all of our
senses believe that we are complete. What if that is not
true? When I was young, TVs were black and white.
Then along came color and a whole new world opened
up. What if there are senses that we are missing now
but will acquire later on? There are some who claim
that they have a sixth sense. What if that is the precur-
sor of what is to come? If so, then a whole new world
will open up as well and what was unseen will be seen.

Just as a day is light and dark, our existence consists of the seen and the unseen. When we fall asleep, we
cease to see, hear, feel, touch, or taste. Yet, nothing disappears just because we fell asleep. Even while awake,
just because we do not see something does not mean
that it is not there. Our physical discernment is limited
to a small band of frequencies beyond which we cannot
perceive. Some believe that if something is not subject

to our senses, then it does not exist. But these senses have their limitations. We know this because we use tools to enhance our capabilities: microscopes, telescopes, binoculars, hearing aids and other devices. We function within limits and are dependent on the tools we use to extend the boundaries of our limitations. Our naked physical senses detect certain wavelengths, but not others, and even though we can extend these limits via tools, they are still limited. Our eyes can see, but only within a limited range of vibrations. So it is with hearing, smell, taste and touch.

Our tools, however, are improving. It was not until 1665, when Robert Hooke studied the dead cells of cork with a crude microscope that we realized the cellular structure of tissues. In 1674, Antoni van Leeuwenhoek devised double-convex lenses that could magnify objects mounted on pinheads up to 300 times. Leeuwenhoek was the first to accurately describe protozoa, red blood cells and bacteria. In 1677, he described the spermatozoa of both insects and humans. Over time, the light microscope was perfected and objects could be magnified up to the maximum resolution of light. Since the smallest wavelength of visible light is about 4000 angstroms (1 angstrom is 0.000,000,000,1 meters), any object smaller than 4000 angstroms could never be detected using light as the source of magnification.

With the development of the electron microscope in the 1940s, viruses became visible for the first time. Soon we were able to visualize atoms and, through diffraction and other techniques, prove the existence of subatomic particles. Yet, with all of our advances, our understanding is still limited by the tools we use. Even though we have uncovered and learned a lot, much more lies hidden because we lack the appropriate tools to detect and observe them.

Tools alone will not enable us to know it all. There is another side to life, the world of the unseen; a world that we can know intuitively, or indirectly, bypassing our common physical senses. Even though, consciously, we are aware of only what is subject to our senses, we experience the unseen as well. We experience energy fields, abide by natural laws such as gravity, and are guided by ideals such as justice. These are unseen. The unseen is as real as the seen. They only differ in their dimensionality. While the seen are four-dimensional, the unseen are of a higher dimension existing beyond space/time.

There are three ways to know: directly through the senses, indirectly through the brain, and holistically by way of the heart. Direct knowledge comes through the senses. With our brains we can reason, analyze, conduct tests, and study effects. Holistic knowledge comes through inspiration, intuition and *The Voice Within.*

Finally, the level of our consciousness also limits us. There are many things that exist beyond the four dimensions of space/time. Until we become cognizant of these other dimensions, our knowledge will remain limited. We know of the existence of the unseen. Let us look at some specific examples:

The Human Energy Field

How do we choose our friends? Who are we attracted to or repulsed by? What about instant likes or dislikes? How do we know who to sit next to and who to move away from? What is the basis of human relations? It is the human energy field, or what is commonly known as the aura. The aura emanates from and surrounds each and every individual. It reflects the character, personality, vibrancy, energy level, and degree of health of that individual. We are subconsciously aware of each other's energy fields and interact accordingly. The aura plays a major role in our lives. Yet, we seldom see it physically or are even aware of it consciously. It remains mostly unseen, in the dark, behind the scenes.

Faith, Beliefs, Knowledge, Skills, and Abilities

Each of us has faith, beliefs, knowledge, memories, unique experiences, skills and abilities. None of these is obvious to a casual observer; they are unseen. Often what we value in a human is the seen, the physical. Yet the most important aspects of a human are the unseen: a person's character, personality, skills, abilities, memories, hopes, dreams, relations, knowledge and expertise. None of these are explicit and external. They are hidden and internal. Most people have a philosophy or a faith that guides their everyday living. Yet, faith is nowhere to be seen.

Forces and Laws of Nature

No one has ever seen electricity. Yet, it is a fundamental aspect of our existence. No one has seen the fundamental forces of gravity, electromagnetism, the weak and strong forces in the atomic nuclei, yet we know they exist. We know that nature is orderly and governed by laws. Yet, these laws are never seen. For example, if we want to know the weight of planet Earth, we can use physics and specific formulas to figure it out. The formulas are embedded in nature, but remain hidden. Only the representation of the formulas can be written and seen.

Ideals

Ideals, such as peace, love, harmony, tranquility, and beauty guide our lives, yet they are never seen. For most, love is the most important aspect of the human experience. Countless songs, poems, books and works of art are based upon and dedicated to love. Yet, love itself remains hidden, unseen. Beauty is another ideal. We can see the expressions of beauty everywhere, yet beauty itself remains elusive. We never see it. Justice is an ideal. Our Constitution, the backbone of our laws, is based upon ideals. Ideals are very real, yet they are invisible.

The I, the Self, the Soul

Science has never been able to detect the existence of the I, the Self, or the Soul, anywhere in the body. These three aspects constitute the identity of every human, yet they are nowhere to be seen. The human brain has been examined and studied extensively. There is no I, Self, or Soul in the brain, in the heart, or anywhere else in the body. Our essence cannot be seen, yet its expressions through the body can be seen everywhere. How can we have a continuous sense of self and identity, yet not know where it resides? This is because the I, the Self, and the Soul exist outside of the four dimensions that govern the physical. They do not occupy space. They are unseen.

God

God is the epitome of all that is unseen.

Can we prove that God exists? What is our understanding of God? And what constitutes proof for us? Do we have to see God or angels before we believe in them?

If we are looking for the God of religion with human qualities, we will be disappointed. If, however, we are looking for a transcendent God, then we will see God everywhere. Look for love, joy and beauty and you will see God.

We cannot prove the existence of God directly, but we can do so indirectly and holistically. We see intelligence in nature wherever we look. We see order, organization, beauty, and the majesty of God everywhere.

The Great Unknown

No one knows what lies beyond the perceptible. We are limited to what we can sense physically or what our devices can detect. Beyond that lies the great, mysterious unknown. We are living beings, but our life force, life itself, is never seen. We see and communicate with each other as conscious beings. Consciousness itself, however, is unseen. We breathe air continuously. Yet, we do not see the air we breathe. Is it possible that the seen is an effect, while the unseen is the force and the cause of all that is seen?

Finally, does dark matter exist as unseen?

SPACE

Space: the final frontier. These are the voyages of the starship Enterprise. Its five-year mission: to explore strange new worlds. To seek out new life and new civilizations. To boldly go where no man has gone before!

— *Star Trek*

What is space? Space is defined as "a continuous area or expanse that is free, available, or unoccupied." (Smart Lookup). This does not tell us much. We can only know space by studying what it contains. There is inner space and there is outer space. While inner space is confined, outer space is boundless, limitless and immeasurable.

There is also "mental space" where we do our thinking, reasoning and analysis. It is also where we imagine, visualize and project. Mental space is where we dream and where our dream figures move and have their existence.

To exist is to occupy space. We try to limit space by creating structures that contain us, such as houses, buildings and cities. We think we are isolated in our confined areas; we are not, for everything exists in the same boundless space for space pervades all.

Physically, we appear to be solid. In fact, we are mostly space. Atoms are the fundamental building blocks of the universe. We know that atoms are made up of a proton and a neutron core surrounded by an energy field of electrons. Electrons move so fast that the space between them disappears. The space between the protons and the electrons, relatively speaking, is vast. In other words, atoms are mostly space. Since everything, including us, is made up of atoms, everything is mostly space.

Space appears as an empty nothingness, but it is not. It contains everything, both seen and unseen. Space and time are intertwined. That is why it appears that space can be annihilated with tremendous speed. It is fascinating to observe a ceiling fan. When it is off, it is easy to see the blades and the spaces between them. Once the fan is turned on, the spaces between the blades disappear. The faster the speed, the less obvious the spaces become.

Annihilation occurs when an electron and a positron meet. Similarly, when matter and anti-matter meet, the result is annihilation. Annihilation also occurs when two identical waves, travelling in opposite directions, meet and cancel each other out. Is the result of annihilation nothingness or space? Electrons, positrons, matter and anti-matter exist and are energy. They cannot disappear through annihilation, for energy cannot be destroyed. Annihilation must end up in space that is not nothingness, rather an undetected, yet persistent field of energy, perhaps in the form of electromagnetic and gravitational waves.

Here is something to ponder:

The result of annihilation appears to be a nothingness, an empty space. In mathematics, zero seems to be a nothingness, just like annihilation. When -1 and +1 are added, the result is zero, a seeming nothingness. In fact, any amount added to its equal and opposite amount results in zero. This is akin to adding matter to anti-matter.

Zero is the result of two components, equal amounts of positive and negative. Empty space is the result of two constituents, matter and anti-matter. In the same way we can separate a zero into equal amounts of plus and minus, we should be able to separate nothingness, or empty space, into two components with opposite polarities. Theoretically, we should be able to separate space into an electron and a positron or matter and anti-matter. Once we learn how to do this, we will have free and unlimited energy. From energy we can get matter, and from matter we can form all else. We can do this anytime and anywhere, for space is ubiquitous.

I am always intrigued by how the unseen can give rise to the seen. Water, which we see, touch, taste, and use, is essentially oxygen and hydrogen, neither of which we can see. How can two gases give rise to material water? Is it possible that space is full of undetected energies that give rise to all that exists? I believe that space cannot be empty. It is the abode of the multidimensional. All types of forces have their residence in space.

We need space to move, to place objects, and to exist. Space is unseen, yet it is a witness to all that is and all that has ever been. We exist in space and space exists in us. Just like God, space is everywhere. Space is the great unseen. It is full of potential. It is the final frontier, if we could only discover and master its secrets.

If space is defined as "a continuous area or expanse that is free, available, or unoccupied", then space can be filled. We can fill it with whatever we create. If space is boundless, limitless and immeasurable, then so is our potential. Like space, our divine potential is vast, available, and eager to be actualized. Through imagination and creativity, we actualize our potential. We make the invisible, visible. We fill space with our creations.

CONSCIOUSNESS

Our normal waking consciousness, rational consciousness as we call it, is but one special type of consciousness, whilst all about it, parted from it by the filmiest of screens, there lie potential forms of consciousness entirely different.

— *William James*

I am looking at my legs, lying side-by-side. The left and right legs are not identical. They are, however, amazing in their symmetry, exact mirror images of each other just like gloves that only fit the correct hand. Not only are my legs a mirror image of each other, so are my arms, eyes, ears, face and many other body parts.

How is this achieved? How can one fertilized cell, dividing and multiplying, achieve this symmetry? There must be an overall "supervisor" that oversees the entire process of development. There is. It is a field known as consciousness.

What is Consciousness?

Being is a trinity of:

1. Mass/Energy
2. Space/Time
3. Consciousnes/Life

These three are eternally intertwined and coexist in different ratios. While mass/energy is material and space/time is immaterial, consciousness is the active principle that can act on matter/energy in space/time to mold the material into forms and imbue them with life. Since we are part of being, we too are a trinity of mass/energy, space/time and consciousness/life. Each individual is a different configuration of these three. As we grow and unfold, these configurations change. Of the three, consciousness is the most essential for without consciousness, there is no witness to existence. Without witness, there can be no meaning or sense to being.

Until the advent of quantum physics, consciousness had no place in science. Then it was discovered that consciousness impacts DNA and the behavior of light. Perhaps because of its spin or polarity, consciousness has unique qualities. It organizes matter and imbues life into it. Since consciousness is energy, it is neither created nor can it be destroyed. It is eternal.

The entanglement of consciousness with complex matter gives rise to life, awareness, and mind. Mind is a set of tools in highly evolved beings that consciousness uses to enhance living and bring about progress. A few of these tools are thinking, reasoning, imagination and visualization. Life is characterized as awareness, both internally, within the mind, and externally, within the world. Living beings have a vast potential to metabolize, grow, reproduce, respond to stimuli, and adapt. For a detailed description of the functions of life, please refer to my book: *A Passion for Living, a Path to Meaning and Joy*.

Our lives are a reflection of our consciousness. Consciousness creates and shapes the reality we experience. It is magnetic, attracting experiences into our lives according to its nature. This is based on where we are in our growth cycle and the experiences we need to continue to grow. Once we are high enough on the ladder of consciousness, we experience its latent capabilities of **The Voice Within**, **inspiration**, **creativity**, **imagination**, **clairaudience** (perceiving what is inaudible), **clairvoyance** (perceiving things or events in the future or beyond normal sensory contact) and **clairsentience** (perceiving or feeling things beyond normal sensory contact).

In humans, consciousness manifests as a trinity of:

1. Conscious
2. Subconscious
3. Superconscious.

The Conscious

The conscious is our wakeful awareness. It is where we do our thinking, reasoning and analysis. It is where we use our will, intentions, judge and discriminate. The conscious is the gateway to the subconscious and the superconscious. From this perch (our conscious), we can shape our circumstances and impact our world.

The conscious can be directed toward anyone, any place, or any time. We can direct our conscious to the various parts of our bodies to heal, to energize, and to rejuvenate. We do this by simply intending to do so and then directing our attention there. This very morning, I was carrying a cup of coffee that was full to the brim. It was my intention to keep my hand steady and prevent the coffee from spilling. The results of our intentions are clear in our daily living. Intention is the force that makes it possible for us to walk, speed up or slow down, or decide to stop. To see birds in flight is to observe intention at work. Intention focuses and directs the energy of our conscious into specific channels. Clarifying our intentions and controlling our thoughts and feelings is like placing a guard at the entrance of our temple, the mind. By selecting and monitoring what thoughts and feelings we allow into our minds, we take charge of our lives and determine its quality.

We are much more than our conscious. We have a vast subconscious and a limitless superconscious. If consciousness is like an ocean, our conscious is only a small portion of this ocean. It is our immediate surroundings, what we are aware of and able to use. The conscious is the tip of a vast iceberg resting on an enormous subconscious and engulfed by the limitless superconscious.

The Subconscious

The subconscious is the storehouse of all of our automated functions and long-term memories. It houses our deep-rooted fears and desires, and all that we want to forget about. Our emotions rise from the subconscious based upon what is stored there. Our subconscious is fertile soil. Our thoughts, feelings, decisions and intentions are like seeds that drop into this soil. What sprouts and grows influences and shapes our lives. Obviously, not all of our thoughts, feelings, and decisions are conscious. In fact, we live most of our lives unaware of the reason behind the decisions we are making. We walk, talk, breathe, digest our food, eliminate our waste, build our cells and tissues, fight germs, broadcast and receive messages, and carry on innumerable other activities based on subconscious instincts, decisions and intentions. The more we learn to use our conscious to selectively cultivate the subconscious, the more focused and powerful our lives become.

Each night as we go to sleep, our conscious moves to the background while our subconscious moves to the foreground. Our conscious returns when we wake up. During brain trauma or when anesthesia is applied, the brain is forced to go to sleep and the conscious departs the body. Hence, our conscious can function only through the brain, and only when the brain is sufficiently developed and healthy. The subconscious and the superconscious, on the other hand, exist independently. They function on an ongoing basis. The subconscious continuously directs our automated functions even when traumatic injuries affect the nervous system.

The Superconscious

We exist in the superconscious and are engulfed by it. Our superconscious is part of the universal consciousness. By merely tapping into our superconscious, we can touch and influence all consciousness. Our superconscious communicates with us via synchronicities, dreams and *The Voice Within*. We achieve heightened creativity when we learn to access the superconscious. We do this by learning to meditate, and by mastering imagination, visualization, concentration and contemplation. These tools can be used individually or in combination with each other. The most powerful method to access the superconscious is to use our imagination during meditation to actively paint a vivid picture of what we want, and then release it, be passive, and wait expectantly for its manifestation. The answer could appear from any source: as synchronistic (concurrent) encounters, guidance through a dream, inspiration, or an inner urge for a specific action. Listening to *The Voice Within* is receiving messages from the superconscious.

RAISING OUR CONSCIOUSNESS

No problem can be solved from the same level of consciousness that created it.

— *Albert Einstein*

The Ouroboros is an ancient symbol of a snake devouring its tail, thus forming a loop which represents an eternal cyclic process. This process is the human experience. We are in an eternal loop of regeneration and self-renewal. When the Ouroboros consumes its tail, it grows beyond its skin, sloughs it off, and is regenerated. As we live, experience, and learn, we accumulate "spiritual capital." Once we attain the required amount, we grow beyond our skin. We slough it off, undergo a change in phase and jump to a higher quantum, a higher rung of consciousness. We are renewed and regenerated. It used to take humans several lifetimes to be reborn into a higher state of consciousness. Many can now accomplish this in one lifetime. When this happens, they are transformed and reborn with a new name. We notice this name change during significant events in Genesis. Abram becomes Abraham, Sarai becomes Sarah, Jacob becomes Israel. They assume a new name as a reflection of their new higher consciousness. Some exceptional individuals can be reborn several times in one lifetime. These individuals are on an accelerated path. The various quanta of consciousness are akin to classrooms ranging from elementary to graduate studies. Many are students in the lower classes with the numbers decreasing as we move up the pyramid. Because we have freedom of choice, we can spend as much time as we like in each classroom. There is no set time or forced moving up or 'graduation' without first having mastered the associated skills.

The Ouroboros is a symbol of our continuous struggle to attain perfection by unceasingly raising the level of our consciousness. We do this as a feed-back loop in an eternal cyclic existence. What is evolving with each reincarnation is the degree of our consciousness.

We are conscious human beings. Consciousness allows us to have "mental space" where we think conceptually, reflect, reason, dream and use our imagination. The more robust this "mental space" is, the greater the consciousness of a human. Consciousness is like a vast ocean of energy. We dip into this ocean of energy via our conscious mind. While our individual consciousness is local, universal consciousness contains the memories, experiences, and knowledge of all living beings. We can tap into universal consciousness and retrieve whatever we want. We can only access and use universal consciousness to the degree that our skills and abilities have been cultivated thus far. Consciousness is like a stepped pyramid extending into infinity. Each of us occupies a step on this pyramid based on where we are in our development. Experts agree that we function at the level of our consciousness. We can raise our level of consciousness through intent, desire and lessons learned from experience.

We are matter/energy, space/time, and consciousness/life. Matter/energy is **what** we are. Space/

time is **where** we are, the arena where we have our experiences. Consciousness is **who** we are. Like an atomic number that identifies an element and determines its properties, the level of our consciousness identifies us. Just as each element has a name based on its atomic number (the number of protons in its nucleus), we have a spiritual name based on the level of our consciousness. By adding protons to the nucleus of an element we can change its identity. We can acquire a new identity and a new name by sufficiently raising our consciousness.

Every species on the planet is in survival mode except for humans. We evolved beyond survival. We developed culture. Culture is a consequence of the evolution of our consciousness. We also have unique traits that are not shared by any other species. This is not due to evolution alone, for plants and animals have existed and have been evolving for as long as humans have, yet they do not possess these same traits. Here are a few of our distinguishing features:

1. We alone have culture, arts, sciences, technology, religions, philosophies, specialized professions, beliefs, superstitions, rituals and ceremonies.

2. We plan, hope, aspire, and dream.

3. We build and shape our dwelling places. We make an art out of cooking and eating. We also exercise for health and vitality.

4. We alone have financial institutions and use money. We alone require clothing to survive in nature.

5. We alone use elaborate tools. We have developed sophisticated physical tools and advanced mental tools, such as reasoning, analysis, inspiration, imagination and visualization.

6. We alone have a sense of fairness, judicial systems, laws, rules and regulations and a police force to enforce these.

7. We alone have freedom of choice. We can choose to stand or sit, talk or be silent.

8. We possess a sense of wonder, amazement, and appreciation. We are touched by beauty, acts of kindness and generosity.

9. We alone reflect on the nature of our existence, the meaning of life and death. We celebrate birth, mourn death, and ritualize marriage.

10. We alone have a sense of humor, cry heartily, laugh with abandon and appreciate a good joke.

11. We experience boredom as a result of repetitive acts. We crave novelty, value and meaning in what we do.

12. We alone are adept at using concepts, metaphors, simile, allegory, and appreciate puns.

I have gone through a tremendous evolution in my consciousness since my days in Syria. Here is what I believe we need to work on to help raise our consciousness:

Areas To Work On

Knowing Vs. Believing

We can believe in our abilities and ourselves. We do not need superstitious beliefs that diminish our power. It is far better to know than to believe. The gateway to knowledge is continuous education. It is imperative to realize that the purpose of living is to experience, grow in knowledge, acquire skills and abilities and contribute to the growth of others.

Knowing Who We Are

We must know who we are – aspects of divinity. We are not feeble creatures born in sin. Neither are we accidents of nature. We are here by choice as embodiments of divinity. We must value our uniqueness, not only liking, but loving ourselves too. Our self-esteem must continuously rise. Our self-image must improve and approach our highest potential, the ideal self.

Knowing Where Authority Lies

Too frequently and easily we give our power to others. We allow external authorities to tell us right from wrong, what to believe, and how to live.

Power resides within us. We have a mind to think, a heart to feel, and inspiration to know. We can consult experts, but the decisions regarding our lives are always ours to make. We must be fearless and not allow organizations to control us through fear. We must be true to ourselves and live up to our highest ideals.

Understanding The Impacts Of Our Thoughts, Feelings And The Example We Are Setting

Just as others influence us, so we influence others. Living as an example is a major responsibility and we should assume that responsibility with humility.

Being Awake

Humans are exceptional in that they have a soul. They have a "piece" of God within them. Our awareness of this presence, however, is gradual. We must wake up to our divine nature through our experiences, and then assume and express it. To do so, requires innumerable awakenings and many lifetimes. Having this God aspect within us makes us unique with added responsibilities. We wake up when we drop the scales of ignorance, superstition, and fear. We must open our eyes, hearts and ears so we may see clearly, feel purely and hear distinctly. The purpose of life will remain a mystery for us as long as our consciousness is earthbound and in the lower dimensions. As we move up the pyramid of consciousness, we see more clearly. Fortunately, our awakening is gradual, allowing us time to acclimate.

When we are fully awake, we will realize that we are responsible for all that we encounter, are multi-dimensional and are co-creators with God. The mysteries disappear. We are no longer in the dark. We see, we know, and we live accordingly.

Mastering The Use Of Our Minds

We must become skilled at using our minds. Thinking, reasoning, imagining, visualizing, concentrating, contemplating, and meditating are our tool kit. These are powerful and potent tools. Once mastered and employed, we can achieve great results with the least effort.

Mastering Engagement And Detachment

Engaging with life full throttle, yet remaining detached from outcomes is a highly valued skill to cultivate. We should always do our best; yet allow the results to unfold without demanding that the will of our ego be done.

Here are a few specific actions we can take to help raise our consciousness:

Actions To Take

Living A Virtuous Life Of Honesty, Humility, Helpfulness And Love

Pure love is of the essence of God. If we practice love, compassion, empathy and understanding toward others on a regular basis, we can raise our vibratory frequency and with it our consciousness. The easiest step toward growth is to love others deeply, purely, and profoundly. It is easier to do this if we remember that the other is just like us, another aspect of the divine.

Living As A Reflection Of Our Ideals

This includes never taking advantage of anyone, avoiding negative emotions such as anger and hate, being generous with our time and love, helping educate and empower others, and being a shining example reflecting our ideals.

Looking For And Appreciating Beauty

Beauty is in everything. We only need pure hearts to see and appreciate it. Expressing gratitude for life and our experiences, sharing laughter and good times with friends and loved ones is something we can all do.

Seeing Wonder Everywhere

Realizing that everyone and everything is a miracle to behold.

Enjoying The Arts In All Of Its Forms

Listening to uplifting music, and reading inspiring books will lift our spirits and help raise our consciousness.

Making Room For Solitude

Practicing reflection, meditation, contemplation and introspection.

Opening Our Minds And Hearts

Asking *The Voice Within* to guide and inspire us on an ongoing basis.

Continuously Learning

Questioning fearlessly, endeavoring to understand and know, examining our experiences for their hidden value, and extracting valuable lessons from them.

Traveling

Experiencing our beautiful planet with its various cultures, environments and life forms.

Above All, Being True To Ourselves

Our allegiance should not be to systems, institutions, leaders or teachers, but rather to *The Voice Within* and our conscious, realizing that our obligation is to acquire knowledge, not to serve organizations. This entails learning from everyone, taking the good we find and leaving the rest behind, and living like a bee floating from flower to flower, gathering nectar wherever we find it.

Being Active In Spiritual Organizations

Working together with others to promote shared values brings about faster manifestations. It helps everyone grow faster and mature sooner.

Having Aha Moments

Savoring unusual and impactful experiences, such as the birth of a child or the death of a loved one.

There is no question that our consciousness is evolving. What was normal in the past is no longer acceptable. Priests who molested children are now being exposed. Powerful people who abused women are now going to jail. Bill Cosby is in jail. The powerful movie mogul, Harvey Weinstein, was sentenced to 23 years behind bars. Rich people who used their wealth to have their offspring admitted to elite colleges are being exposed, and some of them are going to jail. The old normal is no longer accepted. The power and brightness of light is expanding and dispelling more and more darkness. Our collective consciousness is on the rise.

PART THREE

◆ ◆ ◆

ARRIVAL

SOUL

Rocks and waters, etc., are words of God, and so are men. We all flow from one fountain Soul. All are expressions of one Love.

—*John Muir*

The body is a temporary abode. The soul is the permanent resident. Our soul is our ultimate reality. It is who we are. The soul is the most enduring "treasure" we have. In its basic form, soul is "the breath of God". It is what animates us. Basic soul is what we start life with. Yet, as we live and experience, we augment our basic soul with our individuality and imprint it with our uniqueness. We confer an identity on it and it becomes us, unique and individual. I call these personal additions "Epi-soul."

The first time I realized there were two parts to soul was after I had a motorcycle accident as an adolescent. The second time was after I recovered from my Near-Death Experience (NDE) as an adult. To have a better understanding of these two aspects of soul, we can compare them to computer software. The operating system would equate to basic soul; the various specialized software we use are the epi-soul.

Basic soul gives us our rudimentary functions to survive. We can breathe, move about, digest our food, recognize familiar faces and experience basic emotions. With basic soul we are always in the present moment just as animals are. We are unaware of the past and cannot project into the future. **Epi-soul is what makes us human.** It is the storehouse of our accumulated knowledge, experiences, character and personality. As the epi-soul grows, we begin to wield our ability to choose. With a developed epi-soul, we have advanced memory, are aware of the past and can project into the future. We can develop and use advanced mental tools such as reason, analysis, inspiration, contemplation, visualization, imagination and meditation. We can also have highly developed emotions such as the positive emotions of hope, gratitude and joy and the negative emotions of fear, anger and frustration.

We are a work in progress, a book being written. To go from concept to finished product is a long and arduous process. There are multiple iterations to go through. Additions and subtractions must be made. Sentences and paragraphs must be moved around. The work has to be edited. It takes time and effort, but once we have the final product, then it is all worth it. This is akin to birthing, which involves effort, pain and ecstasy when the "baby" is born.

Creating our epi-soul is similar to creating an encyclopedia of many volumes. We start with soul, a gift from God. As we live and experience, we write on soul and start personalizing it. In each lifetime, we add to our epi-soul. Some add a sentence, others add a paragraph and a few add a chapter. As the epi-soul grows, individuality becomes progressively evident. We begin to remember and function as unique entities.

Knowing this, we can reason why we do not remember anything before birth, or what happens after we die. Just as we do not remember our infancy because the brain and the nervous system have to develop first, we do not remember our pre-birth. Our epi-soul must reach a certain level of development before we can have these functions available to us.

Unlike our basic soul, which is changeless, our epi-soul changes and grows with our experiences. Each experience leaves an imprint on our basic soul. As our experiences accumulate, the imprint becomes more vivid and distinct. Slowly, a unique "image" emerges that becomes our individualized personality. We are progressing toward conscious immortality.

The epi-soul goes through the same developmental stages as we do. In its infancy, we have no memory of ourselves. We do not have the tools to remember who we are – unique expressions of God. In its childhood, the epi-soul has rudimentary abilities, simple memory and undeveloped knowledge of itself. As an adolescent, epi-soul has good memory, but very little self-knowledge. As an adult, epi-soul begins to remember and know itself. When fully mature, epi-soul is completely personalized with total awareness, complete memory and a unique individuality. It is Christ-like.

Experiencing is the means by which we build our epi-soul. It is how our eyes open; we begin to see, understand and know. Knowing who we are goes far beyond understanding who we are. We must function accordingly, for to know is a transformative event. When Adam "knew" Eve, a child was born to them. This is why Mary asked the angel: "How shall this be, seeing

I know not a man?" (Luke 1:34). To get pregnant, she must know a man first.

While our basic soul has the imprint of our source, God, the epi-soul must have our personal imprint. The answer to the question, "Why are we here?", is now clear. We are here to create our epi-soul and attain conscious immortality. We do this by living and experiencing. The more diverse and impactful these experiences, the faster the epi-soul grows and matures. The epi-soul is what makes us unique individuals, each with a distinct name, personality and identity.

To survive death as individuals, we must make our epi-soul strong enough, or developed enough, to retain its individuality or else it will be absorbed into source as a component of the celestial soup. To indelibly impress on our epi-soul, an experience must be intense, repeated several times, and the duration long enough. A variety of experiences are required to develop a balanced epi-soul. Reincarnation provides us this opportunity through cyclic existence. Cycles are not meant to be mere repetitions. Instead, they give us ongoing opportunities to take advantage of circumstances not recognized before to learn from and master. This is why reincarnation plays such an important role. It enables us to grow and mature over a long period of cyclic existence. With each lifecycle, we have an opportunity for different experiences that add to our epi-soul. With each cycle of life, our epi-soul grows until a critical turning point is reached and a change in phase takes place. Just as accumulated variations give rise to new species, our accumulated "spiritual capital" propels us to a higher state of being. We are born anew on a higher plane. We are given a new name. We begin to know who we are, where we came from and can determine where we want to go.

Seeking the treasures that do not spoil is seeking the kingdom within. The kingdom within is our epi-soul and must be built by us. We are our own creators. What we create within as epi-soul is what we take with us when we die. The epi-soul is akin to Christ's "seed", "yeast", "hidden treasure", "fine pearl", and a "net". It has the greatest transformative power. With a mature epi-soul, we are Christ-like. We are individualized children of God.

IDENTIFICATION

*Things can be really empty in this world, and I
don't just mean the music world. It can become a
very meaningless place if you don't really understand: 'Who am I? Why am I here? What am I
doing?' To feel fulfilment and have a deeper level
of understanding, personally, that is the most
important thing.*

— *Alicia Keys*

Who are you?" What would you identify yourself as? Some would identify themselves by
referring to their nationality, religion, lin-
eage, or profession. I am an American. I am a Christian.
I am Italian. I am a lawyer. In early 1972, when I was
seeking my first job in the medical field and not suc-
ceeding, my brother offered me a career in computers.
I rejected it by saying, "I am a Biologist. I do not do
computers." It is true that my education and training
were in the biological sciences, but should that identify and limit me? Later on, I learned to throw away
the shackles that imprisoned me, free myself from my
history, and declare that I am a creative being capable
of anything that I set my mind to. In fact, years later,
I ended up with a career in information systems, using
computers.

The answer to the question, "Who are you?", can limit and imprison us or it can set us free. Obviously, we are different things at different times and no one category fully defines us. When I was a child in Aleppo, Syria, I believed in a rigid form of Christianity and had other restrictive beliefs. I was very limited then. I did not remain a child, or in Syria, and slowly I broke free from my restrictive beliefs.

Growth is the law of life. Growth is not mere expansion. It should be a change for the better. If we do not grow, we stagnate or regress. Stagnation breeds germs and disease, and eventually leads to death. Guided by our inner light and a desire to seek knowledge, we are sure to sustain growth.

Many of us have comfort zones that we do not venture beyond. By placing ourselves in shells, we limit our freedom and stop our growth. By breaking free of our limiting shells, we can continue to grow. By shedding our "skin" of ignorance, we open ourselves up to limitless possibilities. There is no end to growth. As long as we are alive, we can continue to learn and grow. Our divine potential is beyond measure; therefore, we should not place any limitations on ourselves by accepting a fixed and restrictive identity. Our identity is temporary and malleable, and should change easily to adapt to our new adventures.

We are who we believe ourselves to be. We have the freedom to recreate ourselves by constantly learning and growing and being whomever we choose to be. Transformative growth experiences force us out of our comfort zones. They build our epi-souls and allow us to renew ourselves. Because we have a choice, why not choose to identify with our deepest core, our divine essence? Who are we? We are children of the divine, capable, creative and in charge of our own destiny. We are the creators of our evolving selves.

WHO AM I?

Then Moses said to God, "If I come to the people of Israel and say to them, 'The God of your fathers has sent me to you,' and they ask me, 'What is his name?' what shall I say to them?" God said to Moses, "I AM WHO I AM."

— Exodus 3:13-14

I AM who I AM is a translation of the Hebrew: ehyeh 'ăšer 'ehyeh, which can mean "I am who I am", "I am what I am" or "I will be what I will be" or even "I create whatever I create". God is whatever God wants to be.

Christ, on the other hand, was more specific about who He was. He said the following:

"I am the light of the world."

Again Jesus spoke to them, saying, "I am the light of the world. Whoever follows me will not walk in darkness, but will have the light of life."

John 8:12

"I am the way, the truth, and the life."

Jesus said to him, "I am the way, and the truth, and the life. No one comes to the Father except through me.   *John 14:6*

"I am the resurrection and the life."

Jesus said to her, "I am the resurrection and the life. Whoever believes in me, though he die, yet shall he live.   *John 11:25*

God is the great I Am. Jesus is the light, the way, the truth, the life and the resurrection. I choose to emulate both. God is my source and Christ is my example. I, too, can be whatever I choose to be, within limits, based upon my current abilities.

I, too, can say: I Am who I Am for I am part and parcel of the great and only I AM.

I can also say: I am Light for I am consciousness and consciousness is light, which imbues life and leads to knowing and illumination.

Additionally, I can say: I Am The Way for my way is the way of the Higher Self which is part of the Christ Consciousness. My I Am communicates with me as *The Voice Within*. Listening to *The Voice Within* and following its promptings is my way of living.

I can even say: I Am The Truth for all truth is the same. It is the truth that I am an aspect of divinity.

Finally, I can likewise say: I Am The Life and The Resurrection, for the life force within me springs from the Christ Consciousness. It imbues and resurrects my inanimate body into a conscious, breathing, animate, living entity.

Christ was the prototype of what humans can be. How many of us believe that we, too, are just like Him in potential? We can be whatever we want if we believe it, know it, and do what it takes to achieve it. It might require patience, perseverance and may take several steps and innumerable lifetimes before we arrive at our chosen destination.

The goal is *to be*, not to do, not to struggle, but to open our eyes, hearts and minds and realize that, in essence, we already are a singular manifestation of divinity. Each person is a unique vibration of a certain range of frequencies that we can control. The level at which we vibrate determines the state of our being and the level of our functioning.

We are free to choose who and what we are. Our choices are often driven by our heritage and environment. Our choices can also be driven by our awareness and intelligence. We have three instruments with which to make choices: the mind, the heart and *The Voice Within*. We use the mind to think, reason, analyze, compare and contrast. The mind gives us understanding. We use the heart to feel, empathize and sympathize. The heart gives us knowing. *The Voice Within* gives us inspiration, options, comfort and certainty.

These three instruments can be cultivated and employed together. The best use of the mind is critical thinking, which requires detachment. The best use of the heart is compassion, which requires detachment from our ego. To hear *The Voice Within,* requires surrender and detachment as well. The more we employ our minds, hearts and *The Voice Within* in our daily living, the faster we will grow and mature.

"To be or not to be" is not the question, for we always 'are'. The real question is, "What do we decide to be and how do we achieve it?" It all depends on who we think and believe we are.

At our core, our I AM is vibrating and eager to express itself. This I AM, however, is mostly dormant. For most, it is a simple, powerless belief. It can, however, be a realization manifesting as a powerful vibration, a magnetic aura, or a joyous song. This is so when we are awake and in the active phase of expressing our true nature.

Once awakened and activated, our I Am impacts the field of consciousness that covers the globe. We become entangled, imprint and are impacted, by all we encounter. As I traveled the world, my I Am that I Am expanded and spread out. It is not only the universe that is expanding, but also our individual worlds.

The ancients believed that God's name was sacred, secret and unutterable. God, in fact, has three types of names: obvious, hidden and secret names. God's obvious name is what we use to refer to God, such as Deity, Allah, or God. God's hidden name is the collective names of all that exist, especially the people. This is why Christ said:

Then the righteous will answer him, saying, 'Lord, when did we see you hungry and feed you, or thirsty and give you drink? And when did we see you a stranger and welcome you, or naked and

clothe you? And when did we see you sick or in
prison and visit you?' And the King will answer
them, 'Truly, I say to you, as you did it to one of
the least of these my brothers, you did it to me.'
Matt 25:37-40

Finally, God's secret name is indeed unutterable,
for uttering is **doing** while God's secret name is **being**.
The only way to utter the secret name of God is to become. To do this, we must not do for others, but become the others. We do not love; we are love. We do not
seek to be healthy, happy and content; we are. We are
unity and that is the position from which we function.
At this state of functioning, there is no other, nothing
beyond the self. All is the self, our self. We are it and
there is nothing else. From this level of awareness, we
become the Christ Consciousness and with Christ say:

I AM light, I AM life, I AM Love, I AM the way, and
I AM the resurrection. He who has seen me has
seen the Father.

When we function from this level, any thought
we entertain coagulates into a mental and spiritual
seed, a blueprint that, over time, manifests as physical
reality.

THE WORD MADE FLESH

*In the beginning was the Word, and the Word
was with God, and the Word was God. He was
in the beginning with God. All things were made
through him, and without him was not any
thing made that was made. In him was life, and
the life was the light of men. The light shines in
the darkness, and the darkness has not overcome
it.*

—John 1:1-5

I have been fascinated by human speech for a long
time. How do our thoughts translate to the string
of words that we utter? It is so effortless. The invisible eternal ideas become visible, temporal words. The
thought taking flesh and becoming words is analogous
to the Word taking flesh and dwelling among us.

I once gave a seven-hour workshop using notes
written on a few 3X5 cards. Afterwards, I wondered
where did all those ideas and words come from? Where
were they stored? How? The human brain is a marvel to
behold. We are indeed in the image of God.

The ancient Egyptians believed that Ptah created the world by speaking words through his tongue
and by thoughts coming from his heart. Perhaps the

ancient Egyptians got this idea from observing people talk. It is amazing, yet commonplace. Speaking is miraculous indeed. We speak words, but words are symbolic representations of ideas, names, objects, or locations. Since everyone and everything has a name, everyone and everything is represented by a word. Together, we are The Word. The Word that is made flesh is all of creation. Since the Word was from the beginning, and was with God, and in fact was God, the Word is divine. This makes you and me and everyone and everything divine. Even though a word can stand alone, it is much more powerful when viewed in relation to other words in a sentence or paragraph. This is also true of you and me.

In the beginning was the Word – not the words. Singular. In other words, in essence we are all one. We appear different because of the type of word we represent. Before we were made flesh, we were an idea in the mind of God, timeless and eternal. Once uttered, the idea is expressed as word. It is released, separated, is given a name, and independence. It is made into flesh. This separation is what we term The Fall. As we manifest, we take on flesh, become physical, exist in space and time, and we have experiences.

Once we are born, the "umbilical cord", our connection to our source is severed. We become a cell apart from the body. We have independence with freedom of choice. It is up to us to reestablish our connection to the source, the Mind of God. Just as a lone wolf does not have the abilities of a pack, a cell separated from the body, no longer has the body's abilities. It cannot remember or know the body as a whole. Similarly, when the Word separates from the Mind, the Word no longer has the abilities and memory of its source. The instant we are born, we are separated; we lose the memories and abilities of our source. We cannot remember where we came from or know where we are heading. This is true until we develop our individuality, the episoul, sufficiently to easily reconnect to our source and remember.

Christianity teaches that Jesus is the Word. Jesus represents humanity. Jesus is the prototype of our potential actualization. Hence, the reference to the Word can easily be about you and me. You are the Word. I am the Word. We are expressions from the mind of God. Since the mind that expressed this Word can express any word, this Word is generic, representing all words. Hence, if Christ is the generic Word, we are the specific examples of this Word.

The divine in you and me and in everything is not obvious. It is buried within us as seeds full of potential that must intentionally be actualized. Just as Adam and Eve were naked but did not know it, we are imbued and surrounded by the divine but cannot detect it. Unless our eyes, minds and hearts are open, we cannot see the divine in ourselves, or in anyone or anything else.

Survival instincts are ingrained in humanity. We fight, argue and wage war with the intent of winning and defeating our enemies. We live as if there are not enough resources to go around for everybody. We must grow out of survival mode and graduate into cooperation and abundance. Our immediate focus, and often the only concern we have, is our families, our friends and ourselves. We believe we are always the most valuable and proudly state, "Not in my backyard." The fact is no one human is more valuable than another. We are all the "One Word" in different manifestations. Each of us appears as a unique individual because we are at a different stage of growth and unfoldment.

The fact that a word is a symbolic representation of something – be it a person, an object, a place, or an idea – a word is a duality of a symbolic representation and the actuality of what it represents. For example, the name of a person is a symbolic representation of an actual person. The word "apple" represents an actual apple. Similarly, we as a word are both the manifestation and the idea behind our manifestation. Ideas are eternal, while their physical representations are transient. Hence, we are both eternal and transient. We are subject to time only while we are in a material body having temporal experiences. We have a beginning and an end only while we are in a physically manifest form. However, as an idea we do not experience time. We are eternal.

We come to this world as a word. As we live and experience, we add more "words" to our original word. We are in the process of becoming an encyclopedia with many volumes. First, the word must grow into a sentence, then a paragraph, then a chapter and finally, a book before it becomes a volume in our encyclopedia. Each book must go through several iterations where excesses are excised, needed parts added, and improvements enacted. This is a very long and tedious process. The editor-in-chief is the Higher Self where living and experiencing is how we add to our "word", grow and mature.

In the beginning was the Word and this Word was with God. You and I were with God from the beginning. We became flesh and manifested as physical entities. Through us all things are made and without us nothing is possible. We are light, life and love. Our light shines and dispels darkness in the form of fear and ignorance. Our life spreads creativity and growth. Our love baptizes our "neighbors" and transforms them into family.

AS WITHIN, SO WITHOUT

*Never underestimate the power of dreams and
the influence of the human spirit. We are all the
same in this notion: The potential for greatness
lives within each of us.*

— *Wilma Rudolph*

What exactly do we have within us? Humans
are privileged to have a "spark" of the divine within them. This spark is a vast potential. Potential is like a singularity that evolved into
our universe. Potential is like the fertilized ovum that
grew into an entire human. Potential is a seed that became a gigantic tree.

Potential is neutral. It can manifest into greatness. It can also manifest into mediocrity or even evil.
It can remain dormant and does not have to manifest at
all. Looking at my life, I have had and still have numerous paths to actualization. I had the potential to get
killed in one of the wars in Syria. I had the potential to
leave this planet at an early age. I have the potential to
continue growing into maturity.

Consciousness is what directs the path of potential into actualization. We start life with a condensed
sphere of consciousness of the highest vibratory rate.
As this consciousness begins to unfold and expand, it

imbues us with life and makes us conscious beings. Our consciousness is part of Universal Consciousness that pervades existence. This is the kingdom within us that Christ told us to seek. Because we are connected to Universal Consciousness, what we do in our consciousness impacts all else. Therefore, if we want to see change outside, we should start the change inside. That is why we must not hide our light, for if our light shines brightly within, we dispel darkness without. Change must start within us first to see it reflected in the world.

We come to this world as a fertilized ovum, a seed. This is our beginning. Spiritually, we started as a seed as well. All seeds are imprinted, or "stamped", with the image of their source as potential, as a blueprint. This potential can manifest gradually if the seed is planted in good soil and nurtured. Even though humans start their lives as seeds, over thousands of reincarnations and as a result of freedom of choice, individuals take different paths to grow, unfold, and mature. In the process, each develops his or her own unique individuality.

Some seeds fall on "rocks" and between "thorns" and remain dormant. These rocks and thorns stifle the potential of the seeds and prevent them from manifesting their full potential. These rocks and thorns can be institutions, beliefs, traditions or cultures. Other seeds fall on barren soil and hardly have a chance to grow. This barren soil could be any stifling or repressive environment. It can also be our closed minds and rigid hearts. Most seeds fall on normal soil and grow gradually. A few seeds fall on fertile ground and grow exponentially. The beauty of being a "human seed" is that we can choose and change our environment.

Our divine potential is a latent power accessed by our intent, imagination, and creativity. These three aspects act on our reservoirs of potential and transform them into manifestations with powerful results. The journey from potential to actualization is simple, yet fraught with the danger of getting lost along the way. Because of freedom of choice, each seed chooses its own path. This makes each seed distinct. Individuals are unique to the extent each uncovers and highlights its uniqueness.

We are imbued with life. The source of our life is the divine spark of consciousness within us. Living affords us the opportunity to metabolize, grow, respond to stimulation, reproduce and adapt. We metabolize not only food, but also experiences. We grow not only physically, but also emotionally, mentally and spiritually. Our response to stimulation can be physical, emotional, mental and spiritual. We reproduce, but can also produce and create.

Left to itself, a seed "knows" how to grow best because that knowledge is imprinted within it. A seed naturally seeks opportunities and attracts all that it needs to grow. This knowledge is instinctive, stored in its DNA. Humans, on the other hand, must act intentionally. They, not only attract opportunities to grow and mature, they can create these as well.

There are two factors that impact the growth of any seed: environment and heredity. Heredity is potential. We inherit a tremendous amount. What manifests, however, is not random. Environment plays a major role in what manifests out of that immense potential. There are two types of environments: external and internal. External environment includes family, locality, climate, education and similar factors. Internal environment includes thoughts, habits, beliefs, attitudes, worldviews and knowledge. Environments are two-edged swords. They can act as a stimulant or as a hindrance. Fortunately, environments can be easily changed. People can move to better external environments. Of more importance is the internal environment we create and foster. While courage, confidence and high self-esteem nurture and nourish the growth of an individual, fear, shame, guilt, anger, and low self-esteem can stifle our growth.

Since the divine within is only potential, manifesting that potential requires situations that foster growth. This growth happens naturally, through living and experiencing pain and pleasure. Challenges are ingredients of growth we must face until we overcome them and become masters of these situations. We impede our self-actualization by resisting, remaining ignorant and by blindly following. We hasten our growth by being determined, thinking freely, and living fearlessly.

Just as it is the destiny of the seed to grow, bear fruit and reflect the nature of its source, so too our destiny is to manifest our full potential by realizing and becoming the divine being that we are. When the tiny seed finally becomes a mature tree, it will attract all sorts of birds to nest in its branches. It will produce a bounty of fruit to nourish the hungry. It will provide shade and shelter to the weary. When we become who we are meant to be, we will realize that our circumstances are mere reflections of our mind and our reality is a creation of our consciousness. When we finally are a mature "tree" with massive branches, flowers and fruit, we showcase our true nature. We have become who we are meant to be. Now everyone can see us, know our name, and hear our song.

He put another parable before them, saying, "The kingdom of heaven is like a grain of mustard seed that a man took and sowed in his field. It is the smallest of all seeds, but when it has grown it is larger than all the garden plants and becomes a tree, so that the birds of the air come and make nests in its branches."

Matt 13:31-32

IN GOD'S IMAGE

Men create gods after their own image, not only with regard to their form but with regard to their mode of life.

— *Aristotle*

Several religions teach that we are created in the image of God. What does it mean to be created in the image of God?

Does God have arms, legs, and a head?

Does God have emotions, thoughts, dreams, hopes and aspirations?

Does God get sick, hungry, afraid, sad, and happy?

Does God sleep and wake up?

Does God age and eventually die?

If the answers to the above questions are no, then we cannot be in the image of God as physical entities. If, on the other hand, the answers are yes, then God is in our image and not the other way around. So, what does it mean to be made in the image of God?

The best way to understand what it means to be created in the image of God is to stand in front of a mirror. As we do, we see our image reflected back to us.

If we move, so does the image. The image appears to look just like us, but there are substantial differences. For one thing, we are 3-dimensional while the image is 2-dimensional. But the most important difference is that even though the image appears to move, it does not have a life of its own. It does not have any power of volition. If we talk, the voice seems to come from the image, but the words are really coming from the real subject, from us.

As long as we stand in front of the mirror, we are connected to the image. The image remains visible, moves and imitates us. Once the connection is severed, the image disappears. So, it is with us. Our life and abilities emanate from the divine source. As long as we remain connected to that source, our soul or the divine spark within us, we live.

Another simple way to understand what it is to be made in the image of something is to consider a TV program. Imagine that you are watching a basketball game. You might be caught up in the action of the game and believe that what you are experiencing is real and actually taking place on the screen in front of you. You might believe that the images are real, moving, and the players are shooting the ball into the hoop. Because you hear the sounds and the voices, because you see the actions taking place right in front of you, you may be inclined to forget yourself and perceive the events as real.

Now suppose that someone unplugs the power cord. Suddenly, you are back in reality. You realize that the images were a mirage. What you were experiencing were mere "shadows of the real." While the real continues, the images can disappear abruptly. Images have no life of their own. They are mere reflections of the life and activity of the real power behind the scenes.

One last way to understand the concept of being made in the image of God is to look at a seed. A seed is made in the image of the plant it came from. For example, a watermelon seed will produce watermelons, once fully grown. The same is true of a pepper seed or an apple seed. Seeds grow to reflect their source. They are not a replica of their source. A watermelon seed is not a watermelon until it is allowed to grow and manifest its destiny. The same is true of us. We are made in the image of our source and have the potential of our source. We are stamped with the "DNA" of our source and are on our way to fully reflect our source.

To be in the image of God, we must reflect the qualities of God.

1. God is love
2. God is creative
3. God is both the seen and the unseen, the expressed and the potential
4. God is eternal
5. God does not change, but our understanding of God evolves
6. God is One

God Is Love

Just as God is pure and absolute love, so too are we in our essence. God has no judgment, no punishment, no anger, and no jealousy. These exist in us while we are children and in the school of learning and maturing. Once we are fully mature, we will dispense with these qualities and they will disappear, just as we dispensed of our childhood qualities once we grew up. Then we will reflect our true nature without an intervening veil. We will **be** love.

God Is Creative

God is immensely creative, so too are we. Our creativity is boundless. It took humanity a long time to begin to express its ingenuity. However the seeds of inventiveness were always latent within us. Now that we are on our way, birthing new inventions and making groundbreaking discoveries, the pace will quicken. Our creative nature will shine forth and become even more evident. Using our imagination and creativity will usher in spectacular innovations. Slowly, but surely, through creativity, we are manifesting more and more of our divine potential.

God Is Both The Seen And The Unseen, The Expressed And The Potential

God is everywhere, in everything, and there is nothing but God. God is both the material universe and the creative consciousness behind it. The seen aspects of God are the manifest physical world (you and me), while the unseen aspects of God are consciousness and the laws and forces behind these manifestations. So too is our true nature. We are both manifest physical body and the creative spirit behind it, the soul.

God Is Both Eternal And Evolutionary

The unseen aspects of God are changeless and eternal. The seen aspects of God are temporal, cyclic, and evolutionary. So too are we. We have an eternal soul and a physical body, which is temporal, cyclic, and evolutionary.

God Does Not Change, But Our Understanding Of God Evolves

As children, we believed whatever our parents and authority figures told us. We could not think on our own. As we grew, developed and began to mature, we evolved the necessary tools to think independently. When I was young, I had childish beliefs about God. My understanding was limited. Now that I am an adult, I think differently. My childish beliefs were not wrong. They were merely childhood beliefs.

As children, we thought and acted like children. We gave human qualities to our deity. We must not do that as adults. God cannot have human qualities for these are specific to our bodies and the environment in which we find ourselves.

As we live and learn, our understanding of the nature of God will evolve. Our beliefs as children cannot be the same beliefs we have as adults. We are expected to go through developmental stages, experience, learn and improve our understanding. Our march to a better understanding of God must continue.

God Is One

If there is only one God, then this God must be the same God for everyone. There are no exceptions. This God can be viewed and understood differently, but that does not change the nature of God. Christ taught us to address God as our father. This was to show intimacy between members of a family, direct access to God, and our inheritance of all that our father is. God is one. This one is not a single unit. It is a multiplicity containing all.

MY UNDERSTANDING OF GOD

While I know myself as a creation of God, I am also obligated to realize and remember that everyone else and everything else are also God's creation.

— *Maya Angelou*

I do not have a God. God has me, has you, and has everyone else as well. The God I understand is not human, with human features and characteristics. My God is a pure trinity of Love, Joy and Beauty. When I was a young boy, I was asked if God could create a rock so gigantic that even He could not lift it. How human to think of God in those terms! I remember seeing ministers praying to God to protect the soldiers on their way to battle, to kill other soldiers. Can you imagine God favoring one group of his people over another? How human of us!

I used to get angry at God, specifically some of what we attribute to God, which I am sure are not true. I remember a few such instances from when I was a teenager in the monastery studying the Bible. These left an indelible mark on my consciousness. The first one was the killing of innocent children, the firstborn of the Egyptians, as well as the firstborn of livestock:

*At midnight the LORD struck down all the first-
born in the land of Egypt, from the firstborn of
Pharaoh who sat on his throne to the firstborn
of the captive who was in the dungeon, and all
the firstborn of the livestock. And Pharaoh rose
up in the night, he and all his servants and all the
Egyptians. And there was a great cry in Egypt,
for there was not a house where someone was
not dead. Exodus 12:29-30*

What shocked me even more was that God intentionally hardened Pharaoh's heart so he will not let the
people go. And then he punished him with ten plagues.

*Moses and Aaron did all these wonders be-
fore Pharaoh, and the LORD hardened Pharaoh's
heart, and he did not let the people of Israel go out
of his land. Exodus 11:10*

The second appalling instance was when God
sent an evil spirit to intentionally create discord:

*And God sent an evil spirit between Abimelech
and the leaders of Shechem, ... Judges 9:23*

Finally, how about favoring one offering over another that gave rise to anger, an anger so intense that it
led to the first murder in the Bible:

*In the course of time Cain brought to the LORD
an offering of the fruit of the ground, and Abel
also brought of the firstborn of his flock and of
their fat portions. And the LORD had regard for
Abel and his offering, but for Cain and his offer-*

ing he had no regard. So Cain was very angry, and his face fell. Genesis 4:3-5

When we were babies, we suckled milk until we developed teeth. Now that we are adults, we must put aside our childish ways and our infantile beliefs. We must reexamine what we accept and believe.

The fear of the Lord is the beginning of knowledge... Prov 1:7

Fear of the Lord, or God, is **not** the beginning of knowledge; expressing the love of God is. People can believe anything they like about God. That is their prerogative. I do not believe in God. I know God as Love, Joy, and Beauty. I know and appreciate beauty as a reflection of God. Anytime I experience love and joy, I know God in my heart.

No one can sin against God. God does not judge our actions. We do. Mistakes are not sins. If we make mistakes, it is all right, for we learn from them. That is how we improve and mature. Many believe that we need to serve and worship God. It is a human idea that God needs anything from us. God is all, whole and complete. The only way to serve God is to serve God's creations, including our beautiful planet.

Jesus said that we have eyes, but do not see, ears, but do not hear. We have scales of ignorance and immaturity blocking our minds, hearts, and *The Voice Within*. By freeing ourselves from fear, evaluating our beliefs, using clear judgment, and listening to *The Voice Within*, we can slowly shed our "scales" to see and hear clearly.

We have many religions in the world, each proclaiming a true God. These religions have seeds of truth within them. However, over the years, religions have become institutionalized, with rigid teachings and limiting beliefs. In their essence, many religions embody universal truths and are compatible.

Hinduism teaches us animism; that God is in everything.

Buddhism teaches us about constant learning and discovery.

Judaism teaches us about having a personal relationship with God.

Christianity teaches us about love and expressing this love as service.

Islam teaches us to surrender to the will of God. The will of God, however, is not only external, or in a book, but internal as well. It is the still, small voice within each of us.

My guides in life are my mind, my heart, my intuition and *The Voice Within*. Many claim to have the word of God as their holy book. I know that nature, and you and I are the works of God. Studying the works of God is the quickest, most reliable way to know God.

LIVING IN TRUTH

If you tell the truth, you don't have to remember anything.

—*Mark Twain*

ruth is different from fact. Facts are demonstrable, quantifiable and verifiable. Truth, on the other hand, depends on a person's perspective, beliefs and experience. Truth is personal, is felt in the heart, and known throughout the entire being. Truth, like gravity, can be known by its effects. The effects of truth are freedom, lightness, and inner knowing. When we encounter truth, it feels right, fits like a missing puzzle piece, and liberates us.

For many, truth is a concept. Truth, however, is much more powerful when it is actionable such as **Living in Truth**. Living in truth is different for different people, often based on their religion. The first person in history, that I am aware of, who used the term **Living in Truth** was Akhenaton, Pharaoh of Egypt. In one of the most beautiful ancient hymns written by him in adoration of the Aton, he refers to himself as *The King living in truth*. Living in truth for Akhenaton meant focusing on simplicity, beauty, peace, family life, and the adoration of his beloved Aton, the giver of life. "Aton, also spelled Aten, in ancient Egyptian religion, a sun god, depicted as the solar disk emitting rays terminating in human hands, whose worship briefly was the state religion." (Britammica.com).

Living in truth for ancient Egyptians meant abiding by the tenets of The Declaration of Innocence (also known as The Negative Confession), a list of 42 sins, which the soul of the deceased had to recite and honestly say it has never committed when it stands in judgment in the afterlife. These declarations included things such as: "I have not been a man of anger. I have done no evil to mankind. I have not inflicted pain. I have made none to weep...". (Ancient History Encyclopedia). The heart (conscience) of the ancient Egyptian was weighed against a feather. In other words, the heart had to be pure, light and unencumbered by any sins of omission or commission. The feather was the symbol of Maat, the Goddess of truth, justice, order, harmony and balance. Anyone living according to these principles was living in truth. Not living in truth had dire consequences for ancient Egyptians. A person's heart was devoured by the demoness Ammit, and that person would die a second death and be completely annihilated from existence. Living in truth, on the other hand, would set the spirit free, living among the gods.

Living in truth for Jews might be abiding by The Ten Commandments and all the other rules and regulations as stated in the Old Testament.

Living in truth for Moslems might entail upholding and abiding by the core beliefs and practices of Islam and The Five Pillars: profession of faith, prayer, alms, fasting, and pilgrimage.

Living in truth for many Christians would be avoiding sins, reciting and believing in the Nicene Creed. Living in truth for other Christians can simply be to Love and to Serve.

All of the above methods of living in truth are noble and commendable if done in the spirit of love and understanding rather than in fear of punishment in the afterlife. While we do not have to recite a Declaration of Innocence to anyone, our conscience will hold us accountable never-the-less. Living in truth for us is living our truth as we know it and feel it in our minds and hearts, and as we are guided by *The Voice Within*. Living our truth is being true to our innate nature which is in the image of God, giving and receiving love, contributing to beauty and exuding and spreading joy. We must leave Earth better than when we arrived.

Many believe that Christ was the truth and that following him is living in truth. This is one way of looking at it. Another way to view this is to realize that by following the light within we follow Christ. Christ is the light of God. Christhood is an extremely high level of consciousness. Hence, the light that is Christ is within us as our divine light. Knowing this and living accordingly is the way to live in truth and to set ourselves free.

When Christ was asked: "And what is truth?" supposedly he was silent. Christ, however, had told us what truth is.

"And you shall know the truth and it will set you free." John 8:32

Perhaps, instead of asking: "And what is truth?" we should be asking: "And what sets us free?" Living in truth will set us free, but only if we allow its light to permeate us and reach our soul. We block the light of truth when we engage in tribalism, fundamentalism, and blind conformity. We also diminish our light if we believe that we are inferior or superior to others, and accept and follow the opinions of others as fact without questioning. Knowing and living the truth will set us free, but it requires that we let go of all that weighs heavily on our minds and hearts. Often, this is negative emotions such as fear, guilt, and resentment. We must also forgive. **Forgiveness** sets us free. It allows us to shed our burdens, and become light. As long as we blame and feel victimized, we remain burdened and enslaved; we are at the mercy of others. Once we let go, we set ourselves free.

In my book, *A Passion for Living, a Path to Meaning and Joy*, I start the chapter titled: "Wake Up" recounting a dream. In this dream, I followed a large number of people into a pool. Once in the pool, I felt trapped. I was unable to lift myself out of the water and set myself free. Soon I realized that there was a "vaulted ceiling" blocking my escape. After some struggle, I noticed a lock that held the "vaulted ceiling" in place. If only I had the key to unlock it, the "vaulted ceiling" would lift and I would be able to set myself free. I looked frantically for the key, but it was nowhere to be found. I struggled mightily, trying to escape my fate. I was desperate to leave the pool and breathe freely. As time passed, I became more and more frantic. I began to shout in desperation, "I want out. I want out of this pool now." I desperately wanted to be free. Just when it seemed there was no way out, I woke up.

The pool in my dream symbolized life. Following the masses without knowing where I was heading, I gave up my individuality and ended up with the fate of the masses. To free myself, I needed to wake up. To wake up, I needed to escape my predicament. To do that, I needed a key. This key was a passionate desire and a clear, focused **INTENTION** to be free. Intention is the "key" that can unlock the "vaulted ceiling," allow me to escape my fate and be free. My desperate desire to free myself clarified and focused my intention which led to my awakening. Now I know that the key to escaping our fate is intention. This intention must be demanding, clear and even desperate. We can know the truth and live it. We can set ourselves free. To do that, we must wake up to who we are. We must desperately want to know the truth with our entire being. We must urgently want to open our eyes so we can see and know. We must bravely accept the truth even if it contradicts our most cherished beliefs. To open our eyes, we must eat of the fruit, like Adam and Eve. We must fearlessly experience life with all its beauty and challenges. Beauty and difficulties will open our eyes. Once our eyes open, we will see clearly and hear distinctly. We will know and live in truth and the truth will keep us free.

LOVE IS POWER

Love is of all passions the strongest, for it attacks simultaneously the head, the heart and the senses.

— *Lao Tzu*

T here is no human love purer and greater than the love of a mother for her newborn. Love is what humans yearn for, without which they never feel complete. It is often the only ingredient necessary to perform wonders, even miracles. Since God is love, then by loving, we recreate ourselves in God's image and become more like God.

Whereas the gods of the old were righteous, jealous, just, mighty, protective, selective, and judgmental, the God of the "Good News" is only love. Whereas the god of the Old Testament had a number of commandments, rules, and regulations humans were expected to abide by as a condition of receiving God's favor, the God of the New Testament, the "Good News" God, has only one request – let love flow.

And he said to him, "You shall love the Lord your God with all your heart, and with all your soul, and with all your mind. This is the great and first commandment. And a second is like it, you

shall love your neighbor as yourself. On these
two commandments depend all the law and the
prophets." Mt. 22:36-40

The only "commandment" we are given is to love
God and our neighbor as we love ourselves. How can we
love God and our neighbor as we love ourselves? First,
we must know who our neighbor is.

But he, desiring to justify himself, said to Jesus,
"And who is my neighbor? Jesus replied, "A man
was going down from Jerusalem to Jericho, and
he fell among robbers, who stripped him and beat
him, and departed, leaving him half dead. Now
by chance a priest was going down that road;
and when he saw him, he passed by on the other
side. So likewise, a Levite, when he came to the
place and saw him, passed by on the other side.
But a Samaritan, as he journeyed, came to where
he was; and when he saw him, he had compas-
sion, and went to him and bound up his wounds,
pouring on oil and wine; then he set him on his
own beast and brought him to an inn, and took
care of him. And the next day he took out two
denarii and gave them to the inn keeper, saying,
'Take care of him; and whatever more you spend,
I will repay you when I come back.' Which of
these three, do you think, proved neighbor to the
man who fell among the robbers?" He said, "The
one who showed mercy on him." And Jesus said
to him, "Go and do likewise." Luke 10:29-37

Our "neighbor" is a metaphor for all of the opportunities we have to do good and express love. We face these daily. These opportunities do not become our "neighbor" unless we act upon them. We must make everyone our neighbor through our acts of compassion, care, and love. Our love baptizes those we touch and converts them to neighbors. If we recognize opportunities for what they are, and take advantage of them to do good, empower, and express love, then we have loved our neighbor as ourselves and fulfilled our responsibility. However, like any skill that we want to develop and master, we must practice this skill repeatedly until it becomes habitual, or second nature.

Loving our "neighbor" starts with loving ourselves. Unless we love ourselves, we cannot love another. We cannot give something we do not have and the best we can offer others is ourselves. Who we love, what we love, and how we love depends on the connections we establish with others. We do this by recognizing similarities and shared traits. Once a mutual trait is recognized, rapport and oneness can be established. Seeing common traits reflected in someone else allows us to relate to them. Then it is easier to love them.

It is best to view love as a verb. In this case, love is a pure vital flow of healing and empowering consciousness. To allow love to flow, all barriers must disappear. It is easiest to do this when we see others for what they are - an aspect of divinity. That is why it is said: "to love another is to see the face of God." (Les Misérables). We love our children and family members because we see so much of ourselves in them. We share the most with our family, especially experiences. If we learn to capitalize on these common experiences with family members and allow love to flow between us, then we can easily develop our capacity to love. Once we love our family, then we can extend love to our friends and neighbors, and eventually to anyone else. We must not only recognize the common traits we share, but also appreciate individuals for their uniqueness. We should notice how wonderful, unique and miraculous each person is.

In a way, loving our neighbor is loving ourselves; for our neighbors are the various aspects of the same divinity that is within us. By learning to love others, we can begin to remove the blinders from our eyes and cast off the illusion of separateness. We are connected and depend upon each other. The more we allow ourselves to love, the less isolated we will feel. Why live in isolation when we can live in a world full of love?

Life on earth is based on cooperation. Everyone impacts everyone else and contributes to who and what we are becoming. We should not seek to love out of fear or expectation of a reward in the afterlife. Rather, we should choose to love because of its transformative potential. Through love we can heal the sick, manifest abundance, and establish peace on earth. To the extent that we infuse our activities with love and allow love to flow freely, we can impact the course of history. By loving, we extend and enlarge ourselves. By joining forces with others, we more than double our singular abilities, for the whole is bigger than the sum of the parts. The more we extend and join with others in bonds of love, the greater our capacity for creativity, productivity and happiness. Just as the power of the brain lies in the ability of its neurons to network, the more we network, the more impactful we become. By sharing our skills and abilities, we learn from each other and speed up our progress and evolution.

When we love, we communicate and commune better with one another. We realize the value of the group. We pool our unique abilities and cooperate with each other. By cooperating, we can specialize and build for ourselves – and for posterity – a new tower of Babel (Bab = doorway/gateway and El = god). We will build this "Gateway to God" gradually, employing people with different tongues or "languages", talents, customs, nationalities, creeds, races, and beliefs. These people will work together for the common good, bound together by love. This new tower of Babel will be at the center of our New Jerusalem, our city of peace, love, and joy.

When we love, we transform our drab earth into a colorful heaven and achieve our ultimate goal, that of regaining paradise lost. When we love, we gain an understanding of our purpose and find meaning in our actions and experiences. We become healthier, happier and live longer. What pure love binds together; no force can separate. When love brings together diverse people with varied languages, no laws, tyrants, or dictators can divide and separate. When, through love, we begin to realize the benefits of cooperation and the value of the group, with all of its diversity, nothing external can "Babel" or confuse us. One of the best ways to work together is to establish joint ventures or projects.

In ancient times people joined together to build a tower, a gateway to heaven. They were stopped short. Their language was sabotaged. They could no longer communicate and work together for the common good.

> Now the whole earth had one language and the same words. And as people migrated from the east, they found a plain in the land of Shinar and settled there. And they said to one another, "Come, let us make bricks, and burn them thoroughly." And they had brick for stone, and bitumen for mortar. Then they said, "Come, let us build ourselves a city and a tower with its top in the heavens, and let us make a name for ourselves, lest we be dispersed over the face of the whole earth." And the LORD came down to see the city and the tower, which the children of man had built. And the LORD said, "Behold, they are one people, and they have all one language, and this is only the beginning of what they will do. And nothing that they propose to do will now be impossible for them. Come, let us go down and there confuse their language, so that they may not understand one another's speech." So the LORD dispersed them from there over the face of all the earth, and they left off building the city. Therefore its name was called Babel, because there the LORD confused the language of all the earth. And from there the LORD dispersed them over the face of all the earth.

> Genesis 11:1-9

It is time to undo this crime against humanity. It is time for us to come together once more, as one people, in the spirit of love and cooperation, to build together. Undertaking joint projects not only brings people together, but also allows everyone to share the rewards. Joint projects are a win-win for everyone. E Pluribus Unum indeed.

TO LOVE AND TO SERVE

Love gives naught but itself and takes naught but from itself. Love possesses not nor would it be possessed; For love is sufficient unto love.

— *Kahlil Gibran*

C hristianity can be summed up in two words - love and service. These are what Christ embodied.

To Love

There is only one happiness in this life, to love and be loved.

— *George Sand*

To love is to get away from our own ego. It is to make another the focus of our attention. Often, love simply happens. Why and whom we fall in love with is not a mystery. We love another because we detect a spark that sets us on fire. We sense a chord that resonates with our being. Often, we are attracted to others because we want to share our journey and, at the same time, we can aid each other's growth. There are many types of love, the most permanent of which is spiritual love. Spiritual love happens when we recognize the divine within the other; when we realize the other has the same essence that we do; and when our love is from the heart and the soul, instead of just the brain. Ordinary love can fluctuate over time. It can grow in intensity and cement our bonds, but it can also diminish, or even morph into hate. Spiritual love, on the other hand, once experienced, is permanent.

There is a difference between recognizing people for **who** they are and seeing people for **what** they are. **Who** they are is an aspect of the divine, while **what** they are is the result of their circumstances. **Who** they are is perfect and permanent, while **what** they are is circumstantial and can change. Focusing on who a person is rather than what that person is makes it easy for us to spiritually love that person.

For many, unconditional love implies loving another as they are, with warts and all. If this were so, how could anybody improve? Parents who love their children do not allow their children to do everything they want. Children must learn boundaries. Adults have to improve. Often, we are not aware of our shortcomings. We require a mirror to reflect our defects back to us. Friends and family who love us and have our best interest at heart provide this mirror. For by improving, we grow and become better. Hence, we should contribute to our brother or sister's well-being and, when called for, point out what we see as areas requiring improvement. This is a service of love. When we point out areas of improvement, we must keep in mind that we cannot have a pole in our eyes while pointing at the straw in another's. We cannot be obese while accusing another of being fat. Compassion and caring are the keys. More importantly, we should take to heart what others suggest about how we can improve ourselves, and act accordingly.

Finally, when we love, we give freely without expecting anything in return. We give gladly. At times, we willingly sacrifice for them. All this means is that until they get on their feet, we put their welfare ahead of ours.

... And to Serve

Now the only way you can serve God on earth is by serving others. — *Rick Warren*

Service is spiritual. We serve to empower. We focus on serving needs and not wants, and to add to another's "Happiness Factor". Christianity is based upon service. When the disciples asked Christ who among them was the greatest, this is what he said:

But Jesus called them to him and said, "You know that the rulers of the Gentiles lord it over them, and their great ones exercise authority over them. It shall not be so among you. But whoever would be great among you must be your servant, and whoever would be first among you must be your slave, even as the Son of Man came not to be served but to serve, and to give his life as a ransom for many." Matt 20:25-28

Giving is an opportunity to serve. When we serve with an "earthly" mentality, selfishly and with an ulterior motive, we lose that which we give. If we give to be noticed, to gain recognition, this would be our reward. However, when we serve with a "heavenly" mindset, freely and lovingly, we gain much more than we give. There is no loss with spiritual giving. It is a recognition that we have been blessed and in turn, we can bless others by serving their needs. Life is balanced. To reap, we must first plant. It is a law of life that, if we receive, we must give back in return. We have received a great deal from our parents, teachers and communities, and we have an obligation to give back. A great way to give back is to serve those in need. It is our responsibility to do our part to help those less fortunate. We can give to take care of other's needs. We can also teach and empower, so that others can grow and achieve independence.

Some serve by giving of their time, skills, and abilities. Others serve by giving money and material goods. What is important is the manner in which we give. We should do it as anonymously as possible. We can give privately, not letting the left hand know what the right hand is doing. The finest gift to give is our attention. The best giving is giving that comes joyfully from the heart.

To give of ourselves – our knowledge, skills, and abilities – we must first possess these. We cannot give something we do not have. The best teachers are those who continue to learn, even if they already know a lot. It behooves us then to continuously work on improving ourselves. The better we are, the better the quality of our service. The more we have, the more we can give. Even living an exemplary life is a form of service. The better example we set, the more impactful our lives can be.

Some religions require tithing, which is mandatory giving. We can also give directly to God's creations, those that we encounter. By loving and serving those that God brings into our lives, we love and serve God.

Love and service are two sides of the same coin. They are eternally intertwined.

WHEN TWO OR MORE
COME TOGETHER

For where two or three are gathered in my name,
there am I in the midst of them.

—*Matthew 18:20*

For where two or three are gathered in my name. How can people gather in the name of Jesus? Is simply saying that they are getting together in the name of Jesus enough? How can a name hold so much power? The literal interpretation of the above statement is that whenever two or more gather in Jesus's name, He will be in their midst (physically). Since this has never happened, there must be more to this statement. I know exactly what this "gathering in His name" means. I have experienced it on many occasions. I used to have a Jamaican friend who loved to engage with me in deep spiritual discussions. Hours would fly by and both of us would be amazed at the insights we would gain. We would have breakthrough understandings. But first we need to know exactly what His name was.

She will bear a son, and you shall call his name
Jesus, for he will save his people from their sins.
All this took place to fulfill what the Lord had
spoken by the prophet: "Behold, the virgin shall

286 | LISTENING TO THE VOICE WITHIN

*conceive and bear a son, and they shall call his
name Immanuel" (which means, God with us).*

Matt 1:21-23

Was his name Jesus or Immanuel? While Jesus
means savior, Immanuel means God is with us. It is
much more appropriate to interpret Immanuel as God
is within us. What is within us is the Christ consciousness that is the light of the world, the way, the truth,
the life and the resurrection. These are what Christ is.
These distill down to the essence of what Christ represents: light of wisdom, understanding, love and service. Hence, this coming together is in the spirit of
light, love and service.

Individuals coming together in the name of Jesus
must **know** that they have Christ within them, must
understand that they are consciousness and that this
consciousness is the light of the world, the way, the
truth, the life and the resurrection. This knowing is
where the power of transformation lies. This coming
together, in the name of Christ, is what saves us. It is
so powerful that it is a sacrament in Christianity – the
sacrament of marriage. Through marriage, two individuals, representing complementary principles, join
together in love. Their joining creates the opportunity
for wondrous achievements, which neither alone could
achieve. This union transforms both and results in creative new births.

This "coming together in His name" does not
apply only to people. It is a universal concept abundantly manifesting in nature as well. Anytime two or
more atoms, elements, organelles, cells, tissues, organs,

systems, individuals, communities, or even countries come together in the spirit of light and love to share, cooperate or even unite, something unique and miraculous happens. *New and unique possibilities are born.* This coming together must be in light and love, involving the giving up of individuality for the benefit of the collective, in service of the higher good.

Where does materiality come from? When an electron and a proton give up their independence and unite in "His name" (love), hydrogen is born. Hydrogen gives rise to all the other elements and matter manifests.

Where does liquidity come from? When hydrogen and oxygen come together "in love" and unite, water is formed; wet, liquid, potable water with unique characteristics, distinct from either hydrogen or oxygen.

Where does salinity come from? When sodium and chlorine come together "in love" and unite, salt is formed.

How can water – two gases, hydrogen and carbon dioxide – combine to become food? **Where does edibility come from?** When gaseous carbon dioxide, and liquid water meet in the leaves of plants, chlorophyll uses the energy from the sun to split the water molecule into oxygen and hydrogen. The hydrogen then combines with the carbon dioxide to form carbohydrates. Chlorophyll then releases the oxygen that we breathe, and without which we cannot survive. Carbohydrates are food we eat.

When a few organelles come together and unite, a new entity, the cell, is born. The cell has incredible capabilities and totally unique qualities. The newly formed cell now has a "home" inside its own membrane, and can ingest food and extract energy. It can get rid of waste and defend itself against attacks.

Just as the progressive merging together of organelles give rise to successively more complex cells, cells come together to form tissues, organs, systems, and the body. The body is capable of far more than any cell, tissue, organ, or system alone. The body exhibits creativity, superior intelligence, and self-awareness.

The next level of organization after the individual is that of the family. Through marriage, two individuals accomplish far more than either could alone. They create a home and raise children. After family comes the community. In a community, individuals come together, giving up their individual separate existence for the sake of the collective. A community consists of various individuals who specialize and contribute ideas, goods, products and services. Our current level of "coming together" is at the country level. Once we transcend this level and rise to the world level, where all countries join, cooperate, contribute and live in peace, we become highly efficient, effective and powerful. Breakthroughs will abound.

One of the best ways to progress on our planet is to cooperate in the spirit of light and love, "in His name". When countries, especially adversaries, undertake joint projects, and appreciate one other, everyone benefits from the breakthroughs and we move closer to peace on earth.

It is light and love that bring individuals together and propel them to form a larger group. Love is the innate realization that whenever two or more come together *in light and love*, creativity will be enhanced and all will realize additional benefits. This inborn realization is the driving force behind cell division and our innate desire to reproduce. In a sense, *the ultimate function of love and sex is to bring individuals together so that new features may manifest.* This innate constant force that propels us to join and unite manifests as desire, attraction, love and lust. Because of these natural forces, life endures and new features continue to be born.

Life progresses from the simple to the more complex, from reactions to purposeful actions, and from the individual to the community. The reason that life is evolving toward more complexity and higher levels of organization is because, through cell division and reproduction, ever-increasing numbers of individuals develop the awareness to interact, unite and bring forth new and original qualities.

Finally, when individuals come together and unite with clear, focused intentions and agreed upon goals, they transform and transmute themselves and the world. This has to be done in the "name of Christ", in the spirit of service, light and love. Then humanity can say to the "mountain", "Move", and the mountain will be gone. They can also say, "Let there be light", and light will shine forth and dispel darkness.

GOOD NEWS AND SAD NEWS

Everyone has inside of him a piece of good news. The good news is that you don't know how great you can be! How much you can love! What you can accomplish! And what your potential is!

— *Anne Frank*

There is the story of a pastor who got up one Sunday and announced to his congregation: "I have good news and bad news.

The good news is, we have enough money to pay for our new building program.

The bad news is, it's still out there in your pockets."

I, too, have some good news and some bad news. The good news is great news, while the bad news is sad news.

The Good News

Jesus went to a synagogue on the Sabbath, opened a scroll, and read the following passage from Isaiah 61:1:

The Spirit of the Lord is upon me, because he has anointed me to proclaim good news to the poor. He has sent me to proclaim liberty to the captives and recovering of sight to the blind, to set at liberty those who are oppressed, to proclaim the year of the Lord's favor. Luke 4:18-19

Christ came to bring us "The Good News." The Good News is in fact great news and it is about us. It is about overcoming poverty, freeing ourselves from bondage, recovering our sight and hearing, and releasing our oppressive burdens. What ails us is not only physical; it is emotional, mental and spiritual as well. We must consider the deeper meaning of "The Good News." There are four parts to the Good News:

The Good News Is That We Can Have An Abundant Life

Christ said that he came so we may have life and have it more abundantly.

The thief comes only to steal and kill and destroy. I came that they may have life and have it abundantly.   John 10:10

We can have an abundant life if we open our eyes, hearts and minds. We must forgo our burdens, ignorance and fears, and we must learn to listen to *The Voice Within.* Christ did not come to die. He came to show us what our lives could be like. We should not allow Christ's life to be in vain. We can have life and have it abundantly. We have great tools to attain that abundant life: powerful, creative minds, freedom of choice and focused intentions. We have an abundant life when our material needs are sufficiently taken care of, along with an abundance of spiritual gifts. These gifts are knowledge, understanding, peace, intimacy and love.

The Good News Is About The Kingdom Of God

> *And when it was day, he departed and went into a desolate place. And the people sought him and came to him, and would have kept him from leaving them, but he said to them, "I must preach the good news of the kingdom of God to the other towns as well; for I was sent for this purpose."* Luke 4:42-43

We know that the kingdom of God is within us as the Christ consciousness. This kingdom is at hand and can be ours if we know where to look for it. It is within us as our essence, as a seed that needs to be tended to. It is a divine spark that we must fan and allow to catch fire. This kingdom is within us as light, life and love.

The Good News Is That We Are The Word Of God

> *for "All flesh is like grass and all its glory like the flower of grass. The grass withers,*

*and the flower falls, but the word of the Lord
remains forever." And this word is the good
news that was preached to you.*

1 Peter 1:24-25

The words of God are not in holy books. We
are the word of God. We are each the word and
work of God.

The Good News Is That We Are Children Of God

Finally, the good news is that we are each a child of
God.

*I will tell of the decree: The LORD said to me,
"You are my Son; today I have begotten you.*
Ps 2:7

We are children of God, indeed. Who else can we
be? This is not only Good News; it is Great News.

The Sad News

The Good News is that we can have the abundant
life; the kingdom of God is within us; and we are the
word, the work and the children of God. This is, in fact,
magnificent news. The sad news is that we do not know
it. Because we have freedom of choice, we have been
shortchanging ourselves. We have been focusing on
what we are rather than **who** we are. This is due to our
habits, upbringing, and culture. For the most part, we
accept a self-image that diminishes our magnificence.
When we have a choice to believe that we can have the
abundant life; that the kingdom of God is within us; and

that we are the word, the work and children of God, why not accept and believe it? When we have a choice to lift ourselves or to put ourselves down, we should choose wisely. We should choose to lift ourselves up. When we have a chance to speak the truth or tell a lie, why not tell the truth? And when we hear another tell a lie, why not speak our truth without condemning the person? Magnificent individuals cannot be complicit with lies, injustice, or cruelty. They do not take sides with individuals or groups, or pit one organization against another. They shine their light and help resolve conflicts. Magnificent people are light workers and peacemakers, for they are known as children of God.

Blessed are the peacemakers, for they shall be called sons of God.   *Matt 5:9*

For many, the Good News is that Christ came to die for our sins and redeem us. Did Christ really come to die? Or, did we kill Him as a result of our ignorance and hard hearts? Does God require a blood sacrifice, that of his son, to forgive us? Why do we choose to accept such beliefs? Why not pick beliefs that empower and ennoble us instead? Why think so lowly of ourselves? Christ came to show us the way to enlightenment.

It is of no use to be magnificent and not know it. To know that we are magnificent is to shine our magnificence wherever and whenever we are. It is to know that all others, regardless of their position, status, or beliefs, are magnificent as well. We are not better than another because we have a better job, a larger home or more wealth. These are our gifts for this lifetime, and they come with responsibility. The more we are given, the bigger our responsibility to use our gifts construct-ively. It is beneath our magnificence to demean others or think less of them. If we diminish anyone else's mag-nificence, we diminish our own. For we are not only our brothers' keepers, we are one family, a family of equals, each with the same divine spark.

Let us not hide our light under a bush. May we shine it from the mountaintop for all to see and be guided by. The Good News is about you and me. It is about our magnificence. May we spread this great news to all corners of the globe.

THY KINGDOM COME!

Pray then like this: "Our Father in heaven, hallowed be Thy name. Thy kingdom come, Thy will be done, on earth as it is in heaven.

— *Matt 6:9-10*

A kingdom is the domain of a king or a queen, of royalty. There are two types of royalty - material and spiritual. Material royalty is distinct and separate from the ordinary people. Royalty is seen as better, loftier, wealthier, more powerful, elite and wise. This creates separation. Royals rule and the rest are ruled. The royals are the masters and the rest are servants.

Spiritual royalty is different. It is all inclusive. If God is King and a spark of God is in me, in you, and in all, then we are all holy, divine and royal. I am royalty, you are royalty, and so is everyone else, because **we are imbued with the divine.** In this kingdom all subjects are aligned to the will of the divine within them. There is no separate will apart from the divine. There is no ego, no comparisons with another, no classification separating us. Each is a different aspect of the same divine. Each is another royal to be appreciated and looked at with awe, wonder and amazement.

The kingdom of God is a kingdom where love rules. Thy Kingdom Come is an invitation for the realization of the divine in all of us to take place and manifest in our daily lives. When we greet another, look at them and say; "Namaste!" This customary Hindu greeting recognizes and honors the divine light in each and every one – the God in me greets the God in you.

THE SECOND COMING

The Seventh Day Adventist Church believes that it was specially chosen by God to prepare the world for the Second Coming of His Son Jesus.

— *Luke Ford*

Many believe in a literal second coming of a physical Jesus Christ. Christian eschatology and messianic prophecies state that He will come in glory to set up his kingdom, judge his enemies, and reward the faithful, both living and dead.

But in those days, after that tribulation, the sun will be darkened, and the moon will not give its light, and the stars will be falling from heaven, and the powers in the heavens will be shaken. And then they will see the Son of Man coming in clouds with great power and glory. And then he will send out the angels and gather his elect from the four winds, from the ends of the earth to the ends of heaven. "From the fig tree learn its lesson: as soon as its branch becomes tender and puts out its leaves, you know that summer is near. So also, when you see these things taking place, you know that he is near, at the very gates. Truly, I say to you, this generation will not pass away until all these things take place...Heaven and earth will pass away, but my words will not pass away.

Mark 13:24-31

I do not believe in eschatology or in a literal second coming. It is impossible to imagine the physical raising of the dead, whose bodies decomposed eons ago, turned into dust, and were perhaps used by plants as nutrients. No human has ever had just one body. Our physical bodies are in continual change, constantly reforming themselves since conception.

Imagine "stars falling from heaven," literally. It will never happen. Stars, like our sun, are much larger than our planet, Earth. Additionally, if there was a physical second coming, it must have already taken place. For it is stated that this generation will not pass until these things take place. I believe in an alternative Second Coming, a spiritual one. What is a spiritual Second Coming?

The First Coming was the birth of Jesus some two thousand years ago. Jesus was the light of the world. He was the embodiment of the Christ Consciousness. The First Coming took place the instant there was the birth of spiritual light, or the Christ Consciousness, in the heart of Jesus. If The First Coming was a single ray of spiritual light, then The Second Coming is the transformation of that ray of light into the sun.

Jesus was the embodiment of love and service. The First Coming took place the moment there was the birth of the spirit of love and service in the heart of Jesus. The Second Coming is the expansion of that spirit of love and service to engulf the globe.

Jesus was the yeast that was placed in the dough of his local community. At that instant, The First Coming took place. The Second Coming is when each of us becomes a yeast, and in turn, leavens all of our communities transforming our earth into our heaven.

Jesus was the "net" of enlightenment cast in His community. He caught a few "fish". This was The First Coming. The Second Coming is when humanity sheds its ignorance and becomes enlightened en masse.

Jesus was the "seed" of divinity dropped into a specific area of the planet some 2000 years ago. The First Coming took place there. The Second Coming is when that seed becomes a gigantic tree that produces fruit containing thousands of seeds.

A dove descended onto Jesus and a voice proclaimed Him to be the Child of God. This dove is symbolic of divine consciousness. This consciousness embodies the **Light** of wisdom, understanding and knowing; the **Love** for self and humanity; and the **Life** force to live, to serve, and to undergo a miraculous transformation from a human to a child of God. The Christ Consciousness, however, did not remain limited to Jesus. It spread. The Second Coming will take place when all of us become like the Christ, Children of God. Jesus said that all that he did, we can do as well and even more. The life he lived and the miracles he performed can be emulated by all.

Truly, truly, I say to you, whoever believes in me will also do the works that I do; and greater works than these will he do, because I am going to the Father.   John 14:12

The Second Coming cannot just happen. It must be actively brought about. We are the agents of The Second Coming. When, or if, it will happen depends solely on us. We must realize that the sun is the combined rays of light that compose it. We must know that we are light, learn how to combine our rays by working together, and shine our light like a sun. When an individual receives the light, that is a contract. This contract obligates us to use our light to illumine the world. Receiving the light is always accompanied by an obligation to use, spread and multiply that light. Just as a seed is expected to grow and produce a multitude of seeds, we must put what we receive into use so that it may grow and multiply.

The light that we currently possess, our knowledge, talents and abilities, love and compassion are the "talents" we are entrusted with. They must be put to good use. We are the trustees. If we do not put these assets to productive use, then even that which we now have and enjoy will diminish and gradually be lost. The parable of the talents is about us. The talents we have, be it one, two, or five, are our current light. We must work to, at a minimum, double that light. The giver of all talents expects this of us. The best way to do this is in loving service of others.

The Second Coming will not happen if enlightened beings remain aloof and alone. We must work together. We can best serve our world and its inhabitants by getting involved. By becoming a potent yeast and by joining with other yeasts, we can leaven the entire dough of humanity. By intensifying our light and by combining it with the light of others, we can illuminate more of our dark world. By purifying our love and joining with the love of others, we can exponentially increase our transformative power. By becoming a potent seed and joining with other seeds, we can grow into gigantic trees producing innumerable seeds that can grow and form our new Garden of Eden.

Christ said:

unless a grain of wheat falls into the earth and dies, it remains alone; but if it dies, it bears much fruit. John 12:24

We are on earth. We either dig our grave or build ourselves a home and a garden. We have a major responsibility to contribute and hasten our transformation, thereby enabling The Second Coming to take place.

The Second Coming is transformational. Christ is the symbol of the First Coming. He transformed Himself from The Son of Man to The Son of God. The Egyptians were aware of transformation. They had a symbol for it, the scarab or Khpheri (the beetle). The beetle transforms itself from an egg to a winged scarab. We transform ourselves when we grow up, mature and cast off our blinders of ignorance, childishness, and fear.

It is our duty and obligation to transform ourselves from being mere humans to Children of God. The first step in transforming ourselves is to be fearless, for nothing extinguishes our light faster than fear. Next, we must learn to control our thoughts and emotions, for they are impactful. They can as easily build as they can destroy.

We can hasten The Second Coming. We are capable and powerful. We are carriers of the genes of the ancients. We are a bridge. We are connected to the past, through our ancestors and to the future, through our children and their descendants. We are a bridge between what preceded and what will follow. We are all of our links and connections to humanity. We are powerful beings. We are much larger than what we initially seem to be. We can impact the whole world and change the course of history.

Christ represents the best of humanity. Metaphorically speaking, to be like Christ we must assume his qualities and consume his personhood by "devouring" him.

> So Jesus said to them, "Truly, truly, I say to you, unless you eat the flesh of the Son of Man and drink his blood, you have no life in you. Whoever feeds on my flesh and drinks my blood has eternal life, and I will raise him up on the last day. For my flesh is true food, and my blood is true drink. Whoever feeds on my flesh and drinks my blood abides in me, and I in him. As the living Father sent me, and I live because of the Father, so whoever feeds on me, he also will live because of me. This is the bread that came down from heaven, not like the bread the fathers ate, and died. Whoever feeds on this bread will live forever."   John 6:53-58

Obviously, we are not talking about eating Christ's physical body and drinking His blood. Rather spiritually and allegorically, for He is "The Bread of Life" and "The Living Water". During The Last Supper, Christ offered his body and blood to us to eat and to drink as a symbolic transfer of his power, knowledge, and abilities. In other words, by assuming Christ's qualities, we become sons and daughters of the Almighty and agents of The Second Coming. The purpose of the Christian communion is to take Christ internally and become Him. By being Christ-like, we are the light, the life, the way and the resurrection. The Second Coming begins with our transformation, and perhaps even our transfiguration.

BRAVE, ENLIGHTENED WORLD

*We need enlightenment, not just individually
but collectively, to save the planet. We need to
awaken ourselves. We need to practice mindful-
ness if we want to have a future, if we want to
save the planet and ourselves.*

— *Thich Naht Hanh*

To be brave, we must be fearless. To be fearless,
we must know that we have nothing to lose.
To have nothing to lose, we must give up our
attachments. To have an enlightened world, we must
leave darkness behind. For too long, we have been
controlled by fear, superstition and ignorance. For too
long we have stagnated at adolescence. For too long,
we have been lost. Just as the Prodigal Son found his
way back to his father, we must find our way back to a
brighter future where cooperation and peace on earth
is the norm.

We are creators. We can create a brave, enlightened world founded on cooperation, knowledge and
love. Reason and inspiration will be our guide and the
light of *The Voice Within* will lead the way. In this
world, there will be no room for barbaric wars and no
squandering of resources. It will be a world where humanity works together for the benefit of all.

We live on a planet where everything is inter-connected and everyone is linked as cells in the body that is humanity. Earth is one. Thus, all that inhabit this earth; humans, animals, plants, lakes, rivers, mountains and oceans are one for they are interconnected. We are the gardeners, caretakers, and guardians of planet Earth.

Many believe that health, wealth and happiness are the goals of life. These are consequences that result from the decisions that we make. We are on earth to experience, to cultivate our unique abilities in service to humanity, and to raise our consciousness on an ongoing basis.

We can have a brave, enlightened world when we value peace, cooperation and friendly competition, above all else. Where we are a lighthouse radiating respect, compassion and understanding. Where every human being is valued. Where joint ventures are the norm. Where health, vibrancy and productivity are valued more than profit. Where freedom is coupled with responsibility. Where the mind is developed to employ reason, analysis, visualization and inspiration. Where the collective consciousness is tapped to help us arrive at solutions.

A brave, enlightened world is a place where learning and improving are continuous. It is a place where parents and teachers are the cultivators of the divine potential within each child; where the pursuit of passions is encouraged; and where natural abilities are allowed to flourish. In this brave enlightened world, we are courageous, inquisitive and creative. Each and every individual is a miracle to behold. Each is like a stone dropped into their environment to generate a beautiful wave to help enrich humanity. Christ referred to us as being "the light of the world." We can choose to hide our light under a bushel or be like a lighthouse shining it like a torch from the mountaintop.

While in the not-so-brave, old world, gods are revered and worshipped; in the brave, enlightened world, people and nature are the center of attention. In this world, the old holidays are replaced with new ones. Christmas becomes the birth of the divine and its full manifestation in humanity. Pentecost becomes the celebration of our own enlightenment. **Assumption** becomes our gradual transfiguration and the continuous raising of our consciousness. We **assume** our sacred **obligation** to express and manifest our divine potential.

The passion, trial, and the crucifixion of Christ will be celebrated as a reminder of the difficulties and challenges life thrusts upon us. Each of us has a cross to bear; yet it is through these challenges that we grow stronger. Education should prepare us for these trying times. Being human means that we will have challenging periods in our lives. Everyone faces difficulties and encounters obstacles. They are part of the human experience and are necessary for our growth and maturation. Difficulties create opportunities for us to help each other and become closer.

Easter and the Resurrection will become a celebration of our ultimate triumph in molding and reshaping ourselves as expressions of the divine and the transformation of our earth into a heaven of our making. It will be a celebration of our rising from the ashes of the old world into a bright, brave and enlightened world.

One of my favorite holidays is Thanksgiving. Being thankful for all of our blessings, fortunes and even our misfortunes. Being thankful for the people in our lives. Being thankful for our incredibly beautiful planet. Being thankful for the human spirit and its achievements. Being thankful for the opportunity to be, to radiate light, and dispel darkness wherever we may find it. Finally, being thankful for our lives, our minds, our bodies, and our individuality, for we are the agents of the brave, new, enlightened world. If it is to be, it is our sacred duty and obligation to make it so.

APOTHEOSIS

Start by doing what's necessary; then do what's possible; and suddenly you are doing the impossible.

— *Francis of Assisi*

We have been journeying for a long time and we still have a long way to go. However, we are almost there. We can see the light at the end of the tunnel. A while longer and we will arrive. When we do, we will find a gigantic mirror. We will look into this mirror. What will we see? We will see our own reflection. We will appear different, almost unrecognizable. Yet, it will be us as we have always been in potential, a true image of who we are meant to be.

At the heart of every religion is the relationship of mankind with God. Almost all religions profess that man is a creation of God. Since God is All, then man must have emanated from the nature of God. However, it is a fact that a human is not like God. Humans are mortal, limited in knowledge and capabilities. Yet, humans are constantly acquiring knowledge, abilities, and power. This progression of a human on the path of evolution and unfoldment was symbolically enacted in Ancient Egypt as the annual procession from the

Temple at Karnak to the Temple at Luxor. The Pharaoh, representing humans, began his procession at Karnak as a man. Once he arrived at Luxor, he was transformed into a God. Even though it is difficult to see how a man can ultimately become a God, it is far easier to envision how humanity can and will one day become like God.

A human is an individual, while humanity is a collective. If humanity is the body, then each human is a mere cell in that body. While the body has tremendously more capabilities than any cell, the cell is, nevertheless, a part of that body and shares its abilities. A human being might never evolve into being God-like on its own, but as an integral aspect of humanity, it can, and will.

Let us take a closer look at the relationship between a cell, a human, humanity and God. A cell has a short lifespan. A human lives much longer. Humanity is **almost** eternal, while God **is** eternal. A cell is weak. A human is progressively becoming more able and potent. Humanity is **on its way** to omnipotence. God **is** Omnipotent. A cell has few and primitive abilities. A human has incredible abilities. Humanity has seemingly marvelous capabilities. God is all-powerful. A cell has an individual consciousness. A human has self-awareness. Humanity has collective consciousness. God is Universal Consciousness.

A cell can reproduce itself. A human cannot reproduce itself. It produces individual cells that can grow into humans. Humanity survives because of the reproductive capabilities of individual humans. Similarly, God does not reproduce itself as other fully-grown gods, only as individual soul seeds with divine potential - "infant gods" with the potential of God-hood.

A cell has local awareness. A human is partially aware of its past and present, with little knowledge of the future. Humanity is very well aware of its past, its present, and has an inkling of its future. God is Omniscient.

A cell is a unit composed of various organelles. A human is an individual composed of cells, tissues, organs, and systems. Humanity is one, yet composed of many cultures, races, languages and religions. God is a singularity manifesting as a multiplicity containing all.

Therefore, humanity is in a much better position to reflect the qualities of God than any individual human. Yet humanity is made up of individuals and the level of their awareness determines the level of the collective consciousness of humanity. How then can each individual contribute to the apotheosis of humanity? By improving the self via three processes:

1. Remembering
2. Activation
3. Resurrection

Remembering

As soon as we are born, the connection to our mother (our source) is severed. At that moment, the connection to our spiritual source is severed as well. We become an individual. We forget where we came from, why we are here and where we are going. We no longer have the same memory as when we were connected. A whole individual has full memory of who he or she is. So does a being in the spiritual world. The moment we separate from our source, we lose our memories. Once we grow and establish spiritual connections to our source, we become whole again. We remember and we know.

Connecting to our source is easier than we think, for our source is not somewhere outside, but within us as our Higher Self. Living, experiencing and listening to *The Voice Within* is how we establish connections to our Higher Self.

We can speed up our remembering by intentionally connecting with our source. We can do this through meditation, contemplation, visualization and imagination. In reality, at no time are we ever actually separate from the source of our spiritually. Separation is an illusion. Even our physical separate individuality is an illusion. We are always connected to everyone. We just do not know it. To have a better understanding on how everything is interconnected, please read: "**The Tomato**," in my book: *A Passion for Living, a Path to Meaning and Joy.*

When the Prodigal Son was living with the pigs longing to eat as they did, he had forgotten who he was. Then he remembered that he had a father, a home, opulence and everything he ever wished for. Remembering **who** he was instead of what he was, he set forth to return home. We, too, must remember **who** we are, return home, and reconnect with our source, the God within, our Higher Self.

Activation

Most of our powers remain dormant. We must awaken and activate the powers that lie within. We can do this by activating or awakening our energy centers or chakras. There are seven major chakras inside the human body. These are:

1. Root or base chakra
2. Solar Plexus
3. Navel
4. Heart
5. Throat
6. Pituitary or third eye
7. Crown or pineal

Each energy center, or chakra, is a vortex and represents a major quality or an ability that we must cultivate, or master, to become Christ-like. These energy centers are activated through impactful experiences. Our trials, challenges, victories and heartaches help us develop the abilities we need to activate our power.

The activation of each energy center requires a critical mass of experiences and mastery. That is why in each lifetime the focus is on one energy center and the mastery of the set of qualities that align with that center. Finally, when all of our centers are activated, we actualize our potential and become a son or a daughter of God.

Mastering the base chakra is progressing beyond survival into thriving.

Mastering the solar plexus chakra is progressing beyond sex into communion.

Mastering the naval chakra is progressing beyond personal power into compassionate and spiritual power.

Mastering the heart chakra is progressing beyond emotions into spiritual love.

Mastering the throat chakra is progressing beyond facts into truth, and becoming skilled at communication, expression, and the art of listening.

Mastering the pituitary chakra is progressing beyond seeing into insight and knowing.

Mastering the crown chakra is progressing into enlightenment, knowing and experiencing oneness. It is living in truth.

The number for mastery is twelve. That is why Jesus had twelve disciples. Each was a symbolic representation of a virtue or quality that Jesus had mastered. Twelve is a symbolic number representing the twelve virtues or qualities that we must master in order to gain full mastery. Once all twelve virtues or qualities are mastered, then we become Christ-like and attain enlightenment.

Resurrection

Resurrection is rebirth. To be born into the new, we must shed off the old. Since apotheosis is transformation, a new humanity must be reborn. We must relinquish the old humanity of wars, barbarism, opportunism, and taking advantage of the weak. We must renounce exploitation and abuse. Instead, we must embrace collaboration, cooperation, trust and appreciation. When we do, we are on our way to maturity. The functioning of the mature humanity must reflect the perfect harmony of the human body, where each part contributes its best and shares in the miraculous and abundant capabilities of the collective.

The story of Osiris, his murder, dismemberment and eventual reassembly is an example of what resurrection entails. Osiris, as a whole body, is alive. Once dismembered, he is dead. Resurrecting Osiris is the act of gathering the body parts or members back together. When all the body parts are put back together, Osiris is brought back to life. This is done by Isis when she re-members all of his body parts.

Therefore, as individual body parts, cells, or independent individuals, we are dead. Once all of our parts are re-connected, we come back to life. When we join together, and re-member, we are resurrected. Resurrection is uniting with our Higher Self, with each other, and ultimately with God.

◆ ◆ ◆

The future of humanity is bright. The pace of our advancement is accelerating. We have come a long way in a very short time. We progressed from kerosene lamps to electricity, from horse and buggy to modern automobiles. We advanced from kites to planes, jets, and supersonic flights. We no longer use the abacus. We have super computers at out fingertips. We landed on the moon and are now going beyond. If in a few short years we have advanced greatly, where will we be in a hundred years? How about in a thousand years? We cannot imagine our future. However, one thing is certain. More and more of our divinity will be evident. We progress from seed to germination, to sprouting, to enduring adversity, to growth, to budding, to blossoming, to bearing fruit. Harvest time is in our future. When that time comes, we will have actualized our innate divine potential. We will have attained Apotheosis.

Apotheosis is the last step of our personal and collective journeys – the final transformation where we reach the pinnacle of power, wisdom, and clarity. We will have progressed from infancy to childhood, adolescence, adulthood, and finally, to maturity. Apotheosis is our reward. We may still have work to do, but we have come to the end of our internal and external struggle and strife. We are home and we are at peace. We have arrived. We are ready to chart the next phase of our own evolution.

EPILOGUE

Is there a plan for our lives? If there is, it cannot be forced upon us by another, not even God. That would encroach on our freedom of choice and the nature of our being. Since we are part of deity, the plan must be of our own making. Prior to being born, we plan the major events of our lives the same way we plan for any long trip. However, unlike any earthly trip, we forget our plans the moment we are born. We are on our own. We must rediscover our purpose. We have excellent tools to use, though: mind, heart, inspiration and *The Voice Within*. It is easy to get lost in the journey of life because of all the distractions our freedom of choice affords us, but there is a lighthouse flashing its light at us to help us find our way. I believe that in addition to our regular self, we have a Higher Self that, when consulted, will provide us with the best personal path to attain our objectives. This Higher Self functions internally, as *The Voice Within*, and externally, as synchronicity.

Synchronicity is "the simultaneous occurrence of events which appear significantly related but have no discernible causal connection." My life is full of synchronicities. These are so wonderful that when I examine them, I am left tongue-tied. I wrote my first book, ***A Passion for Living, a Path to Meaning and Joy***, because of an inner urge from *The Voice Within*. This book, my second, is the result of synchronicities and inspiration from *The Voice Within* as well. Here are three more examples of both being attentive to *The Voice Within* and synchronicity:

1. Going to college was not an option, as I had no money. By synchronicity, I met a lady who barely knew me, yet she loaned me the money and I was able to attend the American University of Beirut.

2. I spent two years in a monastery. I had an aversion for the military. Yet, when I heard the advertisement: "Be all you can be, join the U.S. Army" on the radio, I knew instantly that is what I needed to do. I enlisted and, eventually ended up working at Walter Reed Army Medical Center, which began my civilian career.

3. I was not keen on getting married, having witnessed the misery of my parents' marriage. Yet on my first date with Barbara I knew that she was the one I should marry. I clearly "heard" the whisperings of *The Voice Within*, recognized the importance of my "inner-knowing", and I acted accordingly.

How *The Voice Within* and synchronicities impacted my life are too many to enumerate here. Suffice it to say that I would not have the life I do, had I not acted on them. I have been on an accelerated path to growth and maturity. This is because I am in touch with my Higher Self, the one that communicates with me via *The Voice Within* and synchronicity. Obviously, we are free to accept these ideas or reject them. Acting on them, however, makes all the difference in how well we live, how quickly we reach our goals, and how swiftly we mature. Listening to *The Voice Within* is active. It has three main ingredients:

1. We must first ask, knock, insist and persist. We must actively seek the guidance or the answer.

2. We must be attentive, expecting and trusting until the answer comes.

3. Once The Voice Within speaks to us, we must be fearless and boldly act upon its promptings. The more we act, the stronger the line of communication becomes between us and The Voice Within.

This book is a guide for transformation. Use it and become enlightened or ignore it and stay the same. Each of us has a clear choice.

A NOTE TO THE READER

A Gift

What is the best gift you can give to yourself, to the one(s) you love and to those you care for? A gift that is valuable and has the most transformative power. This book is a guide for transformation. It is full of empowering and liberating insights, any one of which has the potential to change lives. Christ stated, "You will know the truth and the truth will set you free." Reading this book will expose many truths. We have been given freedom of choice, but freedom of choice is useless unless we use it to improve our lives and the lives of those who matter to us.

This book is an inspired work. It is a labor of love. It is written to empower, enlighten, and set us free. After reading this book, if you agree that it is what I say it is, could you please let others know about it? They, too, deserve this gift. I sincerely appreciate your help in spreading the word.

Best wishes for transformation and enlightenment,

Shahan Shammas

ANOTHER BOOK BY SHAHAN SHAMMAS:

A Passion for Living, a Path to Meaning and Joy

Table of Contents

For information about Shahan's workshops, seminars, and availability for speaking engagements, please email to:
    shahanshammas@verizon.net

To order **A Passion for Living, a path to meaning and joy**, for $19.95 plus $3.95 S/H. Please email your request to: shahanshammas@verizon.net

Order 2 or more copies and the shipping is free.

ACKNOWLEDGEMENT

I would like to express my gratitude to all those who helped make this book a reality. I would like to start with my wife Barbara for her dedicated support, understanding, and patience, and for reviewing and editing the book. Next, I would like to thank Olivia Barron for her encouragement and suggestions; and Joseph Shammas, Steven and Jeanette Pashigian for their reviews, comments, continued support and encouragement. Finally, a special thanks to Sarah Shellow for her creative suggestions, Betsy Fetchko for her editing and professionalism and a deep gratitude to Emily Duttine for her suggestions, editing and encouragement.

ABOUT THE AUTHOR

Shahan Shammas

Shahan was born in Aleppo, Syria. At the age of 15, he went to Lebanon where he entered a monastery to study and prepare to be a monk. After two years in the monastery, he left to continue his education. Shahan graduated from the American University of Beirut with a Bachelor's degree in Biology. At the age of 24, Shahan left for the United States and became a US citizen after serving three years in the Army. After working as an Electron Microscopist at the Walter Reed Army Medical Center for 7 years, Shahan started a new career in Information Systems at the Treasury Department. After retirement, Shahan taught Life Skills to adults at the Judy Hoyer Family Learning Center for 10 years. Shahan's background is in the Sciences, Religion, Philosophy and Spirituality. Shahan has lectured extensively in the areas of acquiring knowledge, raising consciousness and actualizing the human potential.

BOOKS BY THIS AUTHOR

A Passion For Living, A Path To Meaning And Joy

To live a life of meaning and joy, we must know who we are and how to best take advantage of our circumstances. We must live for a purpose that embodies who we want to be. We can be victimized by our circumstances or we can choose to live the life we want. If we apply the insights in this book, we will wake up, decipher the meaning of life, and master the art of living.

www.ingramcontent.com/pod-product-compliance
Lightning Source LLC
Chambersburg PA
CBHW030911090426
42737CB00007B/161